LUTHERAN
HIGHER EDUCATION

An Introduction for Faculty

ERNEST L. SIMMONS

Augsburg Fortress
Minneapolis

Lutheran Higher Education:
An Introduction for Faculty

Copyright © 1998 Division for Higher Education and Schools, Evangelical Lutheran Church in America.

All quotations from the Scriptures, unless otherwise noted, are from the New Revised Standard Version Bible, copyright © 1989, Division of Christian Education of the National Council of the Churches of Christ in the United States of America. Used by permission.

All rights reserved. Except for brief quotations in critical articles or reviews, no part of this book may be reproduced in any manner without prior written permission from the Publisher. Write to: Permissions, Augsburg Fortress, Box 1209, Minneapolis, MN 55440.

Cover and interior design: Mike Mihelich
Cover art: Koechel Peterson & Associates, Inc.

On the cover is the Seal of Luther.

A full-color version of the seal is described by Eric W. Gritsch in *Fortress Introduction to Lutheranism* (Augsburg Fortress Publishers, 1994):"In the center of the seal is a black cross placed in a heart. The black cross symbolizes Christ's work in the believer, hurting yet healing human nature from the disease of sin. The heart is in the center of a white rose, symbolizing the joy and peace resulting from faith in Christ alone. The white rose is placed in a sky-blue field, symbolizing the heavenly future promised by Christ. Around the sky-blue field is a golden ring, symbolizing the never-ending love of God; it is precious like gold."

Library of Congress Cataloging-in-Publication Data

Simmons, Ernest L., 1947–
    Lutheran higher education : an introduction for faculty / Ernest L. Simmons.
       p.   cm.
    Includes bibliographical references.
    ISBN 0-8066-3849-4 (alk. paper)
    1. Lutheran universities and colleges—United States. 2. Lutheran Church—Education—United States. I. Title.
    LC574.S55   1998
371.071´ 41—dc21

98-8147
CIP
34-38494-2107

The paper used in this publication meets the minimum requirements of American National Standard for Information Sciences—Permanence of Paper for printed Library Materials. ANSI Z329.48-1984.

Manufactured in the U.S.A.

02	01	00	99	98	1	2	3	4	5

Contents

Preface

This book by professor Ernest Simmons begins a series of volumes to be copyrighted by the Division for Higher Education and Schools of the Evangelical Lutheran Church in America. The series will support the scholarship of an Academy of Lutheran Scholars and is dedicated to the memory of Dr. Conrad Bergendoff.

Bergendoff, who recently died at the age of 102, was one of the great Christian intellectuals of this century. He was for many years the president of Augustana College in Rock Island, Illinois. As a young scholar he became involved in the ecumenical movement shaped in part, and brilliantly, by the Swedish theologian Nathan Soderblom. Bergendoff served as his secretary. Throughout his long life he published works that reflected faith and scholarship and the interaction between the two. When he was nearly one hundred, he sent me a copy of his most recently published article on aspects of Swedish immigration in the United States. He was throughout his life an extraordinary example of a liberal-arts scholar whose experience was enriched by the arts, natural and social sciences, humanities, and biblical and theological disciplines. At home in several languages, he brought all of his learning into the life of the church, knowing, as he said, that "we are, and we become, what we hope and what we believe."

It is fitting that this first book in a series to honor Conrad Bergendoff deals with some of the fundamental ideas formulated by Luther. These ideas have helped shape the distinctiveness of Lutheran colleges and universities. At their best, such schools are lively places of learning rooted in the riches of the Christian faith, which seeks rather than fears secular, scientific, and religious knowledge. Dr. Ernest Simmons' work helps those who join our faculties understand core concepts that have enriched the environment of learning and enabled students and faculty alike to move into larger worlds. The late Ernest Boyer once praised the twenty-eight colleges of the Evangelical Lutheran Church in America as rare places in today's world of higher education. He said such schools had found the ability "to probe both the deep places of the mind and the deep longings of the spirit." It is a remarkable compliment. Simmons' book gives us insights into why it can be made.

Dr. W. Robert Sorensen
Executive Director
Division for Higher Education and Schools
Evangelical Lutheran Church in America

Acknowledgments

As with any writing endeavor, this work is the result of the input and effort of many people. While I am responsible for the final product, I do wish to express thanks to a number of people and several institutions instrumental in its coming into being. I wish to thank Concordia College, Moorhead, Minnesota, and its president, Dr. Paul Dovre, for encouraging me to undertake this reflection and for providing the sabbatical leave necessary for its completion. I also wish to thank Pacific Lutheran Theological Seminary in Berkeley, California; its president, Dr. Timothy Lull; and theologian friend Dr. Ted Peters for so graciously providing sabbatical housing, hospitality, and a quiet place in the "Berkeley hills" for writing and reflection.

I owe a debt of gratitude also to the Division for Higher Education and Schools and Drs. Bob Sorensen and Jim Unglaube for their willingness to undertake this project on behalf of the ELCA colleges. I especially wish to thank the members of the Vocation of a Lutheran College Conference planning committee—Drs. Barbara Bombach, Tim Bennett, Tom Christianson, Paul Dovre, DeAne Lagerquist, Phil Nordquist, Ann Pederson, and Baird Tipson—for overseeing and making many productive suggestions in the process of drafting this book. I also wish to express appreciation to my religion department colleagues, especially chairperson Dr. James Aageson, who have suffered through reading several drafts of various chapters. I also would like to thank my editor at Augsburg Fortress, Lisa Gunderman, who has smoothed out my prose as well as helped clarify my content.

Finally, I wish to thank my family: my parents, Ernest (deceased) and Louise, who have given me the gifts of life and love; my wife, Marti, who has been the light of my life and my companion in our educational pilgrimage through life together; and my son, Scott, and daughter, Leah, who are family representatives of future Lutheran college students for whom this endeavor was undertaken in the first place. It is to them that this book is dedicated.

Ernest L. Simmons

Do not be conformed to this world, but be transformed by the renewing of your minds, so that you may discern what is the will of God—what is good and acceptable and perfect.

Romans 12:2

1   An Overview: Why Are We Here?

"Why are you here?" That question was first put to me thirty years ago by a summer guidance counselor as I attempted to preregister for my first quarter at college. It had not been intended to provoke existential anxiety (incoming students have enough of that); instead it had been intended as a pro forma inquiry into my possible course of study. The question stuck, and I have repeated it countless times as my life's journey has taken me to different parts of the world and to the other side of the lectern. That is the question I will use to provide focus for our reflection on Lutheran higher education and the relation of faith and learning. Why are we here? How does what we do at Lutheran colleges and universities differ from other Christian institutions of higher learning or a public university? How are they similar? In this chapter I want to develop a brief rationale for the important contributions I believe Lutheran higher education can provide for our society as well as give an overview of several of the main themes that will be developed at more length in later chapters of this book.[1]

Undoubtedly ours is a time of rapid change and reconstruction at a pace not seen perhaps since the Renaissance itself. In the midst of such uncertainty, very basic questions are asked—questions that lay bare, among other factors, the spiritual nature of our contemporary crisis. The modern concept of pure objectivity in knowing is seriously challenged by the postmodern understanding of the contextual character of all human thought.[2] The Enlightenment separation of fact from value, including the separation of faith from learning and nature from history, is seen by many as having produced a false duality that has wreaked havoc on our ecosystem as well as our society. Regarding education, social critic Neil Postman observes that this lack of a connecting history has resulted in the loss of a "mega-narrative" for our time. There is no coherent larger narrative context into which learning can be purposefully placed. He observes, "Without a narrative, life has no meaning. Without meaning, learning has no purpose. Without a purpose, schools are houses of detention not attention."[3] Religious faith traditionally has provided such a narrative for learning. In effect, this loss of narrative is another result of an objectivism that radically separates faith from learning.

In such changing times it is no surprise that institutions, like individuals, must undertake to redefine themselves. Received definitions and identities no longer speak with the same clarity and eloquence they once did. This is true for both the college and the church. How are these institutions to identify themselves in the emerging postmodern world? What is to be their relationship? Is a common mission to be found? Is symbiosis—life together—a helpful condition for institutions as well as individuals? Behind such questions lies nothing less than the identity of our institutions and the continued engagement of the Christian tradition with contemporary life and thought.

The primary purpose of colleges and universities is to provide a meaningful and effective education for their students. The purpose of Christian higher education is to conduct that education in the context of the Christian faith—faith seeking understanding. Such educational contexts attempt to relate faith and learning and by so doing provide a meaningful narrative for their students. There are, however, many different ways of doing this,[4] so my purpose in this book will be to explore the particularly Lutheran, dialogical way of conducting Christian higher education. **My thesis: The central mission of Lutheran higher education is to prepare students for vocational service to society by maintaining a dialogical interaction between faith and learning. This mission entails helping students develop critical and informed reflection on the nature of the world and the Christian tradition.** To develop this thesis we should look first at the contemporary spiritual crisis of our time and why church-related higher education is important in confronting it. Then we shall turn to models for relating faith and learning that suggest ways of addressing this crisis. Finally we will look at what has been called the "Lutheran difference" in higher education.

For me the great challenge for the future of Lutheran higher education is to keep the questions of faith and learning alive on our campuses. There is too prevalent a tendency to compartmentalize disciplines and to separate faith from learning dualistically. Much of what follows in this book is an attempt to overcome such a dualistic separation. I suggest, however, that we *not* begin this task *from above* with faith being doctrinally imposed and thus stifling critical inquiry and academic freedom. Rather, in a more Lutheran vein, we begin *from below* with the cultivation of a learning environment in which the theological tradition of faith can be encountered.

I invite you to join me in reflecting on this situation in your context, giving it your own personal shape. Up front, however, it is important to say that many diverse responses are needed as we face the educational and social challenges of our time. There is no single way to respond. This book is intended to assist in the shaping process of our reflection. It is not intended to determine its outcome. Premature closure of questions can result only in inadequate answers and responses. I need your help in this task. We all need one another as we attempt to chart a meaningful course for our institutions as we move into the next century.

I. CONTEMPORARY SPIRITUAL CRISIS

From the beginning of the Enlightenment through the middle of the twentieth century it has been common to speak of a separation between fact and value, science and religion, nature and history. Nature, as object, had no intrinsic development but rather was to be understood through scientific analysis in a value-free inquiry in which both human and religious purpose were considered to be irrelevant.[5] History, on the other hand, was the realm of human purpose and religious value in which civilizations rose and fell, charting their courses in dominating an impersonal world. While there are many scholars today who still affirm such a separation, I have come to understand it as a false duality, and I invite you to reflect with me on this observation. Value-free inquiry is not possible for the human knower. Educator Parker Palmer observes that epistemologies have moral trajectories; ways of knowing are not morally neutral but morally directive.[6] Ways of knowing necessarily include ways of valuing, so a complete separation of fact and value is not possible. The challenge is to retain the achievements of objective reflection without perpetuating its limitations.

Although all knowledge is perspectival, not all perspective is knowledge. We can adjudicate truth claims at the same time that we acknowledge their contextual character.[7] Religion requires a view of the world for its expression, and science requires values for the consideration of its applications. History would not exist without nature, and nature itself has a history. Humanity has always connected history to nature through technology and its impact upon the surrounding environment. Many civilizations have fallen because of the environmental destruction they inflicted on their supporting nature.[8] Technology is a prime example of the intentional connecting of fact and value. The values intrinsic in scientific research are given embodied expression through technological application.[9] Today we see this with a clarity that is unprecedented in human reflection, and with it comes an increased responsibility to properly steward such a relation, in effect, to reconnect fact and value and with it faith and learning.

In such a context it is important to point out that a growing number of scholars from various fields consider the present social and ecological crises of Western culture to be fundamentally spiritual and not material struggles. In our time the question of God's existence has been transmuted into the question of meaning, and the search for meaning is a spiritual one. The present quest for spiritual direction is real, with nothing less than human cultural survival at stake. Books ranging from Robert Bellah's *Habits of the Heart*[10] and Cornel West's *Race Matters*[11] to Vice President Al Gore's *Earth in the Balance*[12] all affirm the spiritual and moral character of our contemporary crises. Gore observes, "The more deeply I search for the roots of the global environmental crisis, the more I am convinced that it is an outer manifestation of an inner crisis that is, for lack of a better word, spiritual. ... But what other word describes the collection of values and assumptions that determine our basic understanding of how we fit into the universe?"[13] This spiritual crisis takes many forms as we focus on the human questions of who we are and why we exist.

The human question of "why" always hangs suspended between the finite and the infinite. Juxtaposed between time and eternity, humanity seeks meaning before its own beginnings and after its demise. Part of the grandeur of being created in the image of God, of *humus* (soil) become spirit-breathed and self-conscious, is the ability to ask why. Human beings are meaning-seeking creatures. We are a form of incarnation in which the spiritual is made manifest in the material precisely in the transcending of self-interest.[14] Spirituality is opening up to the needs of the other, to transcendence of the self, and to possibilities of meaning beyond materialistic consumption alone. The study of the liberal arts assists one in opening up to the transcendent dimensions of life and in so doing equips faith for meaningful expression in service to the other. Because of its help in the identity-forming process, there always has been a close connection between liberal-arts education and the Christian faith.

Identity is a process, not a possession, and environment forms identity. Christian colleges must assist this meaning-seeking, identity-forming process by cultivating environments in which faith and learning can be kept in dynamic relationship. Scholarly study and teaching can be understood as spiritual activity, particularly when they are exercised for the good of the neighbor and are an expression of self-transcendence. We are most affected in life by those people who have embodied genuine humanity and faith for us and have opened up our own possibilities to do the same. Spirituality comes through embodiment in the encounter of individual lives as they are given for the needs of others. Spirituality comes through mentoring, lecturing, writing, questioning, listening, and serving—in sojourning with others in the community of inquiry that is academic life. It means being there for others as one incarnates one's own faith in life. It is through personal encounter and experience that education and understanding are born as our mentors assist us in giving rise to thought.

Faith frees the mind for open inquiry and creative reflection, for we are not saved by our own understanding but by the grace of God. Keeping faith and learning in creative relation is a way of directly responding to the spiritual crisis and loss of mega-narrative in our time. Christian colleges have a frontline responsibility in responding to this challenge, but they will not all respond with the same approach.

II. MODELS OF FAITH AND LEARNING

Today the most visible examples of the interaction of faith and learning (reason) are the various ways in which the relation of religion and science have been addressed. Physicist and theologian Ian Barbour talks about the relationship of religion and science in terms of four possible models that also can be seen as distinct ways of relating faith and learning. The four models are conflict, independence, dialogue, and integration.[15]

In the *conflict* model both religion and science are assumed to be asking the same questions, and therefore their responses must be seen as competitive, alternative answers. For example, this would be as true for creation-science advocates as for advocates of scientific materialism. Concordia College philosopher Gregg Muilenberg observes, "In the one case, natural science has been uncritically extended into natural philosophy and, in the other, biblical faith has been presented as natural science."[16] Both extensions involve category mistakes and are destructive and distort their respective fields. In this model faith must conquer learning or vice versa because they cannot peacefully coexist. This is not the way faith and learning are approached in Lutheran higher education.

In the second model, *independence,* faith and learning, like religion and science, are kept separate and are seen as having their own intrinsic integrity. This position has the value of affirming mutual respect but the liability of leaving the two unrelated to one another. As discussed earlier, the separation of nature from history or of fact from value cannot be allowed to persist in our time because of the interconnected, interdisciplinary questions of our age. All thought is contextual and all facts are value laden. Therefore, a complete separation is impossible. This then leads to the third model, that of dialogue.

Dialogue is the intrinsically Lutheran way of approaching the relationship of faith and learning. While each sphere has its own integrity, there is an overt attempt to make connections, to approach their interaction in a constructive manner that is mutually beneficial. The dialogue model requires academic freedom if each side is to have the opportunity to pursue its respective endeavors with integrity. The model also assumes that there are certain types of questions, issues, and concerns that may crossover or intersect. While disciplinary integrity must be maintained, there are questions of ultimate significance that both sides can approach from their respective analyses. Muilenberg observes, "This understanding of the relationship of faith and learning is particularly at home in the Lutheran Tradition where faith is understood as trust in the justifying power of God's grace brought into critical relationship with the other realms of human experience and thought."[17] As will be developed later, this approach to the relation of faith and learning is a direct expression in education of Luther's understanding of the two kingdoms.[18]

It is the educational expression of justification by grace through faith that affirms the goodness and integrity of the creation as well as the finite character of human knowing. Because we are finite, our knowledge is limited and could be wrong. This humble attitude toward knowing requires multiple points of view for self-correction and academic freedom for its expression. Therefore, Lutheran higher education is a strong supporter of academic freedom.

The fourth model, *integration,* deserves consideration as well. In this model religion and science, as well as faith and learning, function in intrinsic complementarity with a common worldview. There are educational traditions, such as the Roman Catholic and the Reformed, which see this as their ultimate goal. The ideal of the unity of truth drives these traditions to bring all understanding into relationship with the Christian worldview under the sovereignty of God. It is a beautiful vision of wholeness, which is certainly an ideal of education.[19] For the most part, however, the Lutheran tradition has opted for a more limited approach, acknowledging that we see only through a glass darkly and that all our thought and action is subject to human frailty and sin. It affirms a dialectic of nature and grace that can mutually inform one another but which in this life never can fully coincide.

Martin Luther struggled with this task in his time. Luther saw clearly a distinction between the world of today (nature) and the world to come (grace). For him these two realms overlapped in the life of the individual believer, not in society as a whole. In the world of today, reason dominates as the means to study the order God has placed in creation. But, following Exodus 33, Luther sees humanity encountering only the back of God in creation, never God's face. Human knowing encounters God through masks, for that is the only way the infinite can enter into the finite without destroying it.[20]

God's new creation, the realm of redemption and hope, stands in tension with the present fallen creation, providing the possibility for creative critique and change. **It is in light of what might be that one can become empowered to challenge and change what is.** Faith and learning can mutually complement one another when held in dynamic relation. It is, in effect, the empowerment of one's baptism for the expression of faith in life. In the educational context it is the expression of baptism through academic vocation.

III. THE LUTHERAN DIFFERENCE

Why are we here? Is there a Lutheran difference in the answer to this question?[21] Yes, Luther's answer is vocation. We are called by God to incarnate faith through vocation as loving service in the midst of the world.[22] Christian vocation is the living out of baptismal faith in the midst of the creation as one seeks to be a "little Christ" to one's neighbor.[23] It is through our work in the world that we incarnate faith and by so doing help sustain the creation. Vocation rejects the separation of the material from the spiritual, of nature from grace, of faith from learning, insisting that they be kept together. Vocation is for the earth and the world of today so that, as Swedish theologian Gustaf Wingren summarizes, "Human action is a medium for God's love to others."[24] The world of today is not a neutral place but rather one of competing and conflicting powers in which struggle is a daily experience. It is for this reason that Luther argued against leaving the world for the cloister, for this would be to abdicate one's calling to serve God against the forces of destruction present in the world.

Why is there Christian education? In Luther's view the fundamental purpose of Christian education was to preserve the evangelical message and equip the priesthood of all believers for service in the church and the world.[25] For Luther and his colleague Philip Melanchthon, one of the direct results of the theological doctrine of justification by grace through faith was public education.

For Lutheran higher education that purpose has not changed, but the manner in which it is carried out must reflect our contemporary context of meaning. The task is to bring into creative interaction relationships of faith and learning as those relationships encounter an increasingly global and multicultural society. The Lutheran model of higher education affirms the importance of diversity and the need to dialogue with multiple points of view. This means that all people are important and contribute to the character of a community of inquiry, including people of other faith traditions. Faculty serve as mentors, co-inquirers, and fellow sojourners in life with their students. Students likewise are co-inquirers and sojourners who assist the faculty in the dialectic of inquiry and the multitudinous ways in which comprehension can be sought. Staff, also, contribute to the community by effecting a conducive learning environment and expressing praise through the quality of their effort and commitment.

I believe that colleges are communitarian, organic institutions, their lives constituted by the cells of faculty, students, staff, and constituents that maintain them. Life grows, it reaches out, it gropes, it crawls, it meanders, for it is always seeking the new niche, the new area for development. Living individuals and institutions do likewise. Diversity within the bounds of a common commitment to connecting faith and learning is not only desirable but sought out, for it can yield creative adaptations that assist mutual survival.

Why are we here? Finally, of course, it is not institutions per se that are religious, but individual believers. It is people who embody mission and incarnate their faith through their vocation. In so doing, alternative possibilities may be envisioned that will constructively critique the present and provide a source for hopeful change in the future. Yale law professor Stephen Carter's *The Culture of Disbelief* raises important points in this regard. For him religion seems to be marginalized as a private affair by the intellectual establishment, thereby undercutting a traditional basis for public morality.[26] In such a "culture of disbelief," Carter argues that God is treated as a "hobby" and anyone who attempts to take religion seriously in public life is treated as a fanatic.[27]

Colleges of the church have a real stake in this discussion, for here, perhaps, if nowhere else in our society, should religious beliefs be raised, discussed, and critiqued in an informed manner that does not dismiss them as a hobby or have to label them as fanatical. Our society desperately needs informed and reasonable discussion of religious beliefs, and our students bring that same need with them when they come to our campuses. To carry on such open reflection on religion is clearly one of the most important contributions Christian colleges and universities can make to the church's mission of enlightened understanding of the faith and educational service to society. In a culture in which public discourse, especially about matters of religion, is not encouraged or even welcome, colleges of the church may offer one of the most effective venues for such deliberations. Our students, our society, and our religious institutions need such reflection.

In this brief overview I have attempted to state a Lutheran dialogical vision for higher education. It has involved a number of elements that must be developed at more length in the remainder of this book. It will be helpful to more fully address both the historical (Chapter 2) and theological (Chapter 3) legacies of Lutheran higher education as background to looking at the character of Christian vocation in the liberal arts (Chapter 4). In light of Luther's understanding of faith, we then will turn to a discussion of the contemporary research regarding student faith development as a window on the differing ways our students respond to the relationship of faith and learning (Chapter 5). We will close (Chapter 6) with a consideration of several major pedagogical issues, ranging from academic freedom and Christian presence to postmodern pedagogy and community ethos. At the end of each chapter there is a section titled "Questions for Reflection" that invites you to connect the material discussed in the chapter to your own context and thinking.

Why are we here? Ours is a time of rapid and widespread change, not unlike the time of the Reformation in the sixteenth century. Reflection on how Luther and, later, Lutheran education responded in their day may be of considerable use to us in our own. Luther turned to the dual resources of faith and learning for uniting both the personal and the social. We are called to go and do likewise, to see what creative educational expressions of the relation of faith and learning are needed and possible in our time of revolutionary change.

QUESTIONS FOR REFLECTION

1. *Why* **are** *you here? What are your primary motivations for being a scholar-teacher?*

2. *How does the academic environment assist you in doing what you seek to do professionally? Personally?*

3. *What relation does your faith commitment have to the academic work that you do? Should it relate?*

4. *Have there been mentors for you in relating faith and learning in your academic career? If so, how have they been mentors? If not, why do you think you have had none?*

5. *Why do you teach at a church-related college/university? If you had a choice, would you remain or move to a public university? Why?*

6. *What activities, resources, programs, and so forth would you find helpful in assisting you in your work at the college/university?*

2 The Historical Legacy

In order to understand where we are at today in Lutheran higher education, it would be helpful to take a brief look at where we have come from and what historical and theological traditions have informed our institutions. The Lutheran church and its educational vision were shaped in a university setting by academicians who were committed to both faith and learning, theology and secular studies.[1] Education was a necessary and natural extension of the reform movement for Luther and became one of the most influential social expressions of the Reformation.

Let us turn to a brief overview of Luther on education and the history of Lutheran higher education before we specifically address the North American context. We shall then turn to a consideration of the issue of Lutheran identity on our campuses today. In the next chapter we will address the major theological themes in Luther's thought and end with a discussion of several models for Christian higher education, which should help clarify the place of the Lutheran tradition in the overall mixture of church-related higher education.

These two chapters then should be seen as parts of a whole covering both the historical and theological legacies of the Lutheran tradition and how together they come to inform an identity and model for Lutheran higher education. Lutheran education in this country began as immigrant education, and we will find that there was diversity in institutional expression practically from the beginning. First, however, let us look at Luther's understanding of education.

I. LUTHER AND LEARNING

As mentioned earlier, justification by grace through faith is the heart of the Reformation for Luther. It is the article by which "the church stands or falls" and is the basis for the priesthood of all believers in which everyone is equal before God. (These theological concepts will be developed at more length in the next chapter.) It is necessary, then, that this priesthood adequately be prepared for the task of expressing faith in life (vocation), which leads not only to an informed clergy but to a civil and informed society as well.

The reality of late medieval Saxony, however, was something less than this ideal. Luther faced strong opposition from his culture regarding sending children to school. The prosperity brought on by the voyages of discovery as well as the influx of Spanish gold into Europe gave rise to a spirit of materialism. The pressure was on to go to work and earn money in the world of trade and industry. Unless they planned for one of the three major professions—law, medicine, or theology—those who went to school were considered "daft" (*Gelehrte sind verkehrte,* which means "the learned are daft").[2] Education was an unnecessary luxury and a waste of time for the average person, so the general population believed. It was much better for a child to learn a useful trade and thus ensure his livelihood.

It is in this late medieval cultural climate that Luther advocates generalized public education for both boys and girls for the first time in Western history. His major treatises on education, the essay *To the Councilmen of All Cities in Germany That They Establish and Maintain Christian Schools* (1524),[3] and his famous sermon *On Keeping Children in School* (1530)[4] are intended to establish not only an educated leadership for the church and government but also an informed laity to serve both the church and society.

The situation was quite serious, for not only had there been limited educational opportunities before the Reformation, but the reform movement led to decreasing support for church-related schools, especially the monastic schools. Some radical reformers (for example, Andreas Carlstadt and Thomas Muntzer) actually were speaking against education, saying that one only needed the Holy Spirit to be fully informed.[5] Many schools were in a state of disrepair and even abandonment as the monasteries closed and their properties and endowments were confiscated by the local authorities. School and university attendance fell off sharply.

At first Luther thought that parents would see to the education of their children, but he soon realized they had neither the training nor the willingness to do so and that drove him to encourage the government officials to establish schools and libraries in their communities. This appeal was successful, with numerous schools being supported and several new ones, including universities, being started (for example, at Marburg, Jena, and Konigsburg). Luther's colleague Phillip Melanchthon oversaw major educational reforms throughout Protestant Germany. In so doing he established the secondary school (*Gymnasium*) between the Latin school and the university and developed the pattern for German university education that has persisted until today. That is why Melanchthon is known as the *Praeceptor Germaniea,* the "schoolmaster of Germany."[6]

These reformers were practical leaders who foresaw the need for education and especially the value of the liberal arts in training for Christian ministry and the life of faith. From the beginning there was a strong connection between faith and learning, building upon the emerging liberal-arts humanism of the Renaissance and the claims to justifying grace of the Reformation. If the Bible is the "cradle of Christ," as Luther referred to it, then surely liberal-arts education, especially language study, is one of the hands that rocks the cradle, through which the Bible is touched, understood, and moved. Luther observes:

> I am persuaded that without knowledge of literature pure theology cannot at all endure, just as heretofore, when letters have declined and lain prostrate, theology, too, has wretchedly fallen and lain prostrate; nay, I see that there has never been a great revelation of the Word of God unless he has first prepared the way by the rise and prosperity of languages and letters, as though they were John the Baptists....[7]

Beyond language study, Luther and Melanchthon both stressed the value of the liberal arts and extolled their beneficial effects in broadening the intellectual horizons and cultural sensitivities of students. In addressing the councilmen of Germany, Luther noted:

> Through the teaching of history children would hear of the doings and sayings of the entire world, and how things went with various cities, kingdoms, princes, men and women. Thus they could in a short time set before themselves as in a mirror the character, life, counsels and purposes, successful and unsuccessful, of the whole world from the beginning; on the basis of which they could then draw the proper inferences and in the fear of God take their own place in the stream of human events. In addition they could gain from history the knowledge and understanding of what to seek and what to avoid in this outward life and be able to advise and direct others accordingly.[8]

Luther also affirmed the teaching of poetry and rhetoric and encouraged the developing natural sciences. Regarding the new methods of observing the natural world, he writes that "we are at the dawn of a new era for we are beginning to recover the knowledge of the external world which we had lost through the fall of Adam. We now observe creatures properly, and not as formerly."[9] Each discipline has its own integrity and value and is not to be subject to another. For Luther and Melanchthon, education was the key to addressing the shortage of pastors and teachers in their time as well as to incarnating the Reformation in daily life.

Luther's commitment to education emerged rather naturally from his own experience. Scholarly investigation, or inquiry, provided the tools by which Luther unlocked "the Book" and discovered the gift of faith. For Luther, that book—the Bible—was fundamental and so, he believed, it should be accessible to all. Thus education became an imperative and led Luther and his colleagues to develop the common schools where education would be made available to all. Indeed, as Luther interpreted Psalm 78:5-6, parents are enjoined to educate children in both divine and human wisdom.

In addition to his personal experience of law and gospel, Luther's commitment to education also was shaped by his doctrine of the two kingdoms. The earthly kingdom of nature, God's left hand, is our place of service, of vocation. The affairs of the earthly kingdom, where one is called to serve the common good (without self-interest), are to be ruled by reason; hence education is essential in order to fulfill one's vocation. God's right hand governs the heavenly kingdom of grace where the Christian is called to be well-informed about the Scriptures in order to express the new life in Christ through faith. Through grace, the Christian lives in both kingdoms and is called to relate to God through faith and make that faith active in love for one's neighbor. As David Lotz writes, in view of Luther's conception of the two kingdoms, it would be correct to depict Luther with the Bible in one hand and "a work of Homer or Virgil or (most fittingly) Cicero in the other."[10] The two kingdoms are to be related dynamically through a life of faithful inquiry.

Closely related to Luther's commitment to the place of inquiry was his commitment to academic freedom. Luther was given the freedom to pursue the truth by his colleagues at Wittenberg and by the princes of the realm. That freedom led him to faith in God's creation of this world and the redemption of humans in spite of what each had become. Indeed, if the world is God's creation, then there is surely no inhibition to the pursuit of inquiry, for any truth discovered is yet another truth about what God has done. In this sense, open inquiry is both privilege and mandate. Within the Lutheran tradition, academic freedom is understood as an application of the doctrine of the two kingdoms to education.

The integrity of creation requires nothing less than the integrity and freedom of disciplines devoted to its study. In the world of today reason dominates as the means to study the order God has placed in creation, thus granting each discipline its own integrity and freedom. As David Lotz observes:

For present purposes it is especially germane to add that Luther not only appreciated the internal integrity of the academic disciplines, but no less recognized and understood their technical autonomy. In a word, he defended academic freedom: the right of each discipline to pursue its specific goals, with its own appropriate methods and conceptual categories, without meddling or interference from other disciplines, including Christian theology.[11]

Luther himself asserts:

No science should stand in the way of another science, but each should continue to have its own mode of procedure in its own terms. Every science should make use of its own terminology, and one should not for this reason condemn the other or ridicule it; but one should rather be of use to the other, and they should put their achievements at one another's disposal.[12]

In Luther's view, reason reigns in the earthly kingdom, and Christ's revelation has no exclusive claim on earthly truth, but human reason has its limits. In this view he parted ways with some of the other reformers and his strictly humanist colleagues.

Luther believed that human reason is subject to error. More importantly, Luther said that while reason is essential and helpful in dealing with matters of faith, such as the heavenly kingdom, it is not definitive. Human reason cannot provide definitive answers to such essential questions of faith as "Who is God?" "What is it to be human?" "What is faith?" Revelation has an essential role in matters of faith, or the heavenly kingdom, and when reason begins to legislate for the heavenly kingdom, when it confuses human justice and the righteousness of God, when it rationalizes divine revelation, then reason becomes "the devil's whore."[13]

Learning cannot redeem the self or the world in a spiritual sense—only God can do that. Perhaps this view is best capsulized in Luther's explanation to the third article of the Apostles' Creed:

I believe that I cannot of my own reason or strength believe in Jesus Christ, my Lord, or come to him; but the Holy Ghost has called me through the gospel, enlightened me with His gifts, and sanctified and preserved me in the true faith.[14]

Reason has its limits. Nevertheless, Lutheran reformers were committed to education, particularly in the liberal arts. For them understanding "the word" required knowledge of language, literature, philosophy, science, and history, of which Luther had a particular interest.[15] This emphasis was continued in the later Lutheran educational tradition.

The great church historian Sydney Ahlstrom describes the flow of the Lutheran tradition as it moved into the post-Reformation period in terms of three currents: the scholastic, the pietistic, and the critical.[16] The scholastic emerged in the context of the fierce debates and religious wars of the late sixteenth and early seventeenth centuries as Lutherans struggled to define themselves against the Roman Catholic Counter-Reformation on the one hand and the Reformed and Radical Protestants on the other. Focusing especially on doctrinal formulation as a way of preserving the Reformation heritage, the scholastic movement argued that Lutheran doctrine could be expressed in formalized statements such as the Formula of Concord of 1580. Richard Solberg concludes that Lutheran scholasticism became rigid and "resulted in finely drawn expositions of Lutheran theology that tended to become intellectual exercises rather than professions of faith."[17]

It is in reaction to this rigid intellectualism that the movement of Pietism emerged in the late seventeenth and early eighteenth centuries, centered at the University of Halle. Pietism emphasized the inner spiritual life and engagement in mission work and deeds of mercy. Less concerned about intellectual formulations, Pietism stressed the commitment of the individual believer in living out an active life of faith and gave a strong impetus to lay involvement in the church.

Finally the critical current emerged in the late eighteenth and nineteenth centuries in response to the rise of natural science and Enlightenment Rationalism. The critical tradition was marked by a sense of intellectual freedom and a desire to ask deep questions and challenge accepted assumptions. This tradition includes such scholars as Kant and Hegel.[18] It is important to remember that this critical spirit that so dominated nineteenth-century scholarship in many disciplines is a direct academic expression of one of the currents of the Lutheran tradition in education.

As we turn to Lutheran immigration, however, not all of these currents would find expression in America. Richard Solberg observes:

> In the migration of Lutherans from Europe to America, however, the "critical tradition" was largely left behind. Most German immigrants in the eighteenth century were peasants and came to a country still in the frontier stage. The few university-trained clergy who came to care for their spiritual needs had been trained in centers of German Pietism. As the supply of European clergy dwindled, the earliest Lutheran ventures in higher education were primarily directed to the preparation of more pastors. Colleges were founded to provide the basic classical languages

necessary for theological study. Thus, a tradition that had been broadly involved in the intellectual milieu of European thought was narrowed to a concern for preparing frontier pastors in an institutional climate strongly flavored by American evangelical revivalism.[19]

Taken together, however, these Lutheran roots suggest a vigorous, open, and free approach to an education in which faith has full sway without ever compromising the freedom or integrity of the academic enterprise. Richard Solberg concludes, "This conviction, that a thorough intellectual preparation of professional leadership for church and community is fundamental to the broad intentions of the Reformation, has provided the driving impulse for higher education within the Lutheran tradition."[20] This connection between education and faith was so firmly planted in the followers of the Reformation that it has lasted for centuries and was carried to other parts of Europe, particularly Scandinavia, and to the New Zion of America through the arrival of immigrants.

II. THE AMERICAN CONTEXT

While this is not primarily a review of the ethnic and social influences shaping Lutheran colleges, those influences are significant and have been considered thoughtfully by several scholars of note. In the case of the Lutheran tradition, I wish to acknowledge a considerable debt to Richard W. Solberg's *Lutheran Higher Education in North America*.[21] In this brief review I will simply highlight some of the signposts and influences that have shaped the vision of Lutheran colleges and universities in America.

Lutheran higher education on this continent has its roots in the German university and the Reformation. Since Luther's place of call was the university, it is not surprising that education was a major agenda for him and his colleagues. Indeed, he and Melanchthon would stir an educational reform movement at Wittenberg that redefined the liberal arts. The universities of the Reformation would become prime transmitters of the Lutheran tradition.

The early Lutheran immigrants to America brought this model along to the new land. There were Lutherans among the earliest colonists, including those who started a Swedish settlement in Delaware where Wilmington now stands and Lutheran members of the Dutch West India Company. The first permanent Lutheran pastor in America was the Reverend Reorus Torkillus, who was sent by the Archbishop of Upsala in 1639, only three years after the founding of Harvard University. He remained until his death in 1691, but there were few other pastors available to replace him. It was this persistent pastoral shortage combined with the need to educate immigrant populations for life in a new land that became the driving force for early Lutheran education. Lutheran education was immigrant-driven education.

The first great Lutheran organizer and pastor in this country was Henry Melchior Muhlenberg, who arrived in Pennsylvania from the University of Halle in 1741. Halle, with its pietist missionary inspiration, would supply more pastors to the early Lutheran churches in eighteenth-century America than any other source. There had been some limited attempts to create schools earlier, but the organization and resources simply were not there, so the schools had to close.

Muhlenberg brought with him the pietist zeal for mission and was also a consummate organizer and mediator. He was installed as pastor of the "United Congregations" of Philadelphia on December 27, 1742. Muhlenberg assisted in the establishment of the Pennsylvania Ministerium, what has been called the most important single event in American Lutheran history, on August 26, 1748.[22] This church structure was to provide the model for most later Lutheran churches during the vast immigrant influxes of the next century. Muhlenberg's legacy was the establishment of structural identity, polity, and liturgy for the Lutheran church in America. With this legacy in place it was left to future leadership to develop educational institutions utilizing the support of this church structure.

The leading Lutheran pastor and theologian at the beginning of the nineteenth century was Samuel S. Schmucker (1799–1873), who was educated at the University of Pennsylvania and Princeton Theological Seminary. He longed to provide Lutherans with a seminary to educate their own pastors. So in 1826, with the help of the General Synod, he established Gettysburg Seminary and became its first professor and president. The need for preparation for seminary education led Schmucker to establish the first Lutheran college in North America—Gettysburg College—in Gettysburg, Pennsylvania, in 1832.[23]

Lutherans, however, have always felt free to argue and debate with one another. Disagreements arose over a number of issues, including what language to conduct education in, what stand to take on slavery (Schmucker opposed it), and how to handle theological issues such as the interpretation of the Lutheran confessions. Schmucker had been concerned about the influence of nonconfessional, nonliturgical, and rationalistic trends on Lutheran churches and thus had established both a college and a seminary that would provide a corrective.

Subsequently, Lutheran Frederick A. Muhlenberg (great-grandson of Henry Melchior Muhlenberg), out of concern for the confessional laxity of Gettysburg, would lead in the founding of the college that would carry his name (1848). On the other hand, Benjamin Kurtz believed that Gettysburg was too formal and confessional and led the establishment of Susquehanna University (1858). Concerns about laxity in confessional matters in the Old World would lead a group of German immigrants to Missouri in 1839, where they would establish a church (Missouri Synod) and a system of education from grade school through seminary.

In other cases the delineations among Lutherans were less theological and doctrinal than they were matters of style or polity. This was especially true among the Scandinavian Lutherans. For example, among the Norwegian Lutherans there were those who emphasized confessional and liturgical matters. They formed the Norwegian Synod and founded Luther College in Decorah, Iowa, and Park Region Luther College in Fergus Falls, Minnesota. Another group was somewhat anticlerical and strongly evangelical. This group formed the Hauge Synod and established an academy at Red Wing, Minnesota. Augsburg College in Minneapolis, Minnesota, reflected the ethos of this movement.

A theological debate among Lutherans on the issue of predestination led to the establishment of St. Olaf College in Northfield, Minnesota, by United Synod pastors and laypeople. Both the synod and the college stood in a meliorist position between the Norwegian Synod and the Hauge Synod and their respective institutions.

There also were social factors that led to the establishment of some of the colleges. The founding of Wittenberg University in Springfield, Ohio, was shaped, in part, by German immigrants who saw their young people being proselytized away by English-speaking revivalistic groups. The founders of Wittenberg therefore determined that an English-speaking college was essential. Luther College, Decorah, Iowa, was founded because of a falling out between the Norwegian Synod and the Missouri Synod over the slavery question.

However important these issues were in the establishment of some colleges, the more significant factor in the establishment of Lutheran colleges across America was the movement of Lutheran immigrants. For example, the Swedish Lutherans would establish Augustana (Rock Island, Illinois), Gustavus Adolphus (St. Peter, Minnesota), Bethany (Lindsborg, Kansas), and Upsala (East Orange, New Jersey). The Norwegians would move from their original base in Wisconsin to Decorah, Iowa; Northfield, Minnesota; Minneapolis, Minnesota; Fergus Falls, Minnesota; Moorhead,

Minnesota; Sioux Falls, South Dakota; Tacoma, Washington; Camrose, Alberta, Canada; and Forest City, Iowa—not to mention all of the academies that were established along the way.

The educational format of the early colleges followed the European model of Latin school, college, and seminary. Wittenberg, established in 1845, would institute the liberal-arts model, a model already developed and well-established on American soil. With the exception of Augsburg College, the Midwestern Lutheran colleges would adopt a similar format. There would be variations in religious expression, academic emphasis, and community styles among the Lutheran colleges and within the ethnic families—variations reflecting particular traditions, both ethnic and religious, as well as local circumstances.

A brief overview of one of the colleges provides a helpful illustration of the pattern for many others. Concordia College in Moorhead, Minnesota, for example, among the Norwegian church bodies of the day, was identified with the United Synod, or the moderate tradition. By 1917 the three major Norwegian church bodies had merged, thus bringing Park Region Luther College and Concordia into the same family. These early Norwegian Lutheran colleges reflected the piety of their parent churches. While the legalisms have largely vanished over time, the concern for community and the evangelistic sense of mission have persisted. As an immigrant college, Concordia's early agenda was similar to its sister institutions: to preserve the values of church and ethnic family while preparing students for effective citizenship in the new land. Again, like many of its sister immigrant institutions, Concordia's early academic program was directed to high-school–age students (the Academy) since the high-school movement had not yet reached the rural areas.

The educational vision of Concordia was determined at the turn of the century when the vocational programs enrolled the most students and a certain faction of the faculty wanted to move toward the academic model of the business college. Another faction of the faculty and influential clergy on the governing board held out for the liberal-arts model that had shaped their education and which they considered the more appropriate model for a Lutheran college. The latter view prevailed and, as the time and needs changed, Concordia evolved into a four-year liberal-arts college, thus affirming the vision of the founders. Concordia's story is typical of Lutheran colleges whose many different factors, both theological and social as well as practical, have come to forge their present identity. It is to the issue of the Lutheran identity of these institutions that we now turn.

III. LUTHERAN IDENTITY

The question of Lutheran identity on college campuses is perhaps the most difficult issue for which to chart a clear and fair direction. There is definitely a dialectical tension here. On the one hand, it is evident from research that Marsden, Burtchaell, Benne, and others (see bibliography) have conducted that the denominational identity of a college is lost when a significant number of both the faculty and student body no longer participate in the tradition. For many schools church affiliation becomes a nice but not necessarily defining descriptor of their life and mission. On the other hand, to dictate fidelity on the part of all faculty and students is to abandon the "Free Christian College" model seen in the Danforth Commission[24] typology as most indicative of Lutheran higher education. (Please see the discussion in the second section of Chapter 3.) Even if not in theory, such practice in reality can create a defender-of-the-faith mentality and ethos that works against free inquiry on campus.

I do not propose here to offer any simple way out of this tension but to see the tension itself as part of the creative expression of the Lutheran tradition. I will argue that Lutheranism, understood as an ecumenical and confessional movement within the church catholic, lives in the dialectical tension between the poles of no church affiliation and denominational ideology. The embodying of this tension is a complex matter involving faculty and student recruitment, campus worship, congregational ownership, and synodical affiliation. There is no magic percentage of critical mass of students or faculty that will or should resolve this tension. Identity is not a possession but a process, a mode of being, a way of engaging in the interaction of one's faith with life. This may be done as effectively by a nonmember of the denomination as by a member. We need denominational diversity on campus not only to enrich our own understanding of the Christian tradition but also to keep Lutherans honest. We need reflective Presbyterians, Roman Catholics, Baptists, Methodists, and others, for they may do more for the effecting of Lutheran identity on campus than a nonreflective Lutheran would. Members of other faith traditions also can contribute creatively to the identity-forming dialectic on campus.

What is at stake here is the desire on the part of the institution to be related to a specific church. Above all else it is a matter of shared intentionality of common purpose. Does a college want to be related to a specific church? As Merrimon Cunningim, longtime president of the Danforth Foundation puts it, the essential point is that "a college must want to be and aim to be so related."[25] A college as a whole must want to be so related to the church and its mission.

As my friend and philosopher William Narum puts it, "Two things are necessary: one, a conscious intention by the college to work for and under the college's relation to the church's mission, and two, a significant measure of congruence among the constituent groups of the college in their understanding of this intention."[26] If the intention indeed be shared, then all participants contribute toward this congruence insofar as there is a commitment to a common purpose. It means that all take part in the embodying of the identity of the school, not by slavish uniformity but by each in their respective way raising the question of church relatedness. Such a shared purpose would not and should not end debate about the embodiment of this intentionality in any given instance—from faculty hiring to campus worship events, for example. But it does place these discussions in the context of mutual commitment and common purpose, which are essential for maintaining identity and trust.

The identity of a faith community always is evolving. It can never be frozen at a particular time or point of embodiment, except at the peril of its own demise. (The Shaker community is an excellent case study in this regard.) Identity comes through continuity of experience and the continually emergent narrative of life shared together. Common, mutually shared purpose is the best way to provide for continuity of identity. This means that identity must be everybody's business or it is not identity at all but rather a nostalgic veneer preserved by anachronistic sentimentality. The Lutheran tradition in higher education by and large has not subscribed to such a narrow vision of education but rather to one of education for service in the world.

Lutheranism is more than a denomination; it is a confessional movement in the church catholic. It is a way of understanding the relation of God and the world characterized by justifying grace embraced through faith. Luther never intended to form a separate church. Rather, he sought to reform the church by clarifying the nature of the gospel through debate in the public arenas of the university and society. In this regard then the character of Lutheran identity began and, to remain vital, must continue to be sustained as a matter of public debate and dialogue within the arena of contemporary intellectual and religious opinions. This is to say that "Lutheran liberal arts" is not an oxymoron but rather an essential statement of the arena in which the character of Lutheran identity is formulated and sustained. It is born of a dialectic between faith and learning.

The constructive challenge for Lutheran identity on our campuses is to continue to maintain such an identity-forming dialectic. Today this dialectic moves between two extremes, both of which I contend should be avoided. At the one extreme is the pole of "no affiliation," pushing religion completely out of the academy as if it is a contagion to academic life. The other pole is "denominational ideology," which seeks to preserve church affiliation by doctrinal imposition and the stifling of creative critique.

For the Lutheran tradition both poles are false and unacceptable alternatives. To gravitate to no affiliation, especially today, flies in the face of the postmodern critique referred to in Chapter 1. (Please also see the more extended discussion of postmodernism in Chapter 6.) There is no academically neutral context for the discussion of ideas. The preferable model is to be self-conscious about one's perspective and social location. At the other extreme, denominational identity has gone to seed when it can no longer creatively engage contemporary intellectual life. If preservation is the only objective, then it is better to acknowledge the demise of a denomination's viability and move on rather than trying to nostalgically retain it by bracketing out critical analysis. The church existed before there were denominations, and it will exist after them as well.

Lutheran identity is forged between these two extremes, in the dialectical tension of what I would call "ecumenical confessionalism." Lutheran identity, if it is to be faithful to what gave it birth, must not simply collapse into denominational preservation nor sell out to some assumed superior position free of affiliation. Lutheranism, understood as ecumenical confessionalism, would resist both extremes. The ecumenical side would prevent denominational ideology by continually reminding the community of the value and presence of other denominational and theological emphases, thus affirming diversity on our campuses. The confessionalism side would argue against the idea of no affiliation by affirming that in the intellectual arena it is preferable to be self-conscious about one's commitments, not assume such discussion is value-free. Such self-conscious confessionalism on the part of Lutherans then frees up others to be self-conscious about their traditions as well. Confessionalism as a dynamic theological expression does not seek imposed doctrinal uniformity but rather a lively and healthy confessional dialogue between traditions.

The freedom of the gospel of God's justifying grace empowers faith for free inquiry. We are not saved by our intellectual or ideological constructions so that we are free to pursue analysis of the world and search for truth wherever it may lead. That is the character of an educational vision that affirms diversity within the overarching unity of God's creation. Born in the liberal-arts setting for reflection on faith and learning, Lutheran liberal-arts education can remain a vital force for sustaining such a dialogue.

QUESTIONS FOR REFLECTION

1. *Do you find any parallels between Luther's time and our own?*

2. *As you reflect on the converging commitments that created our colleges, what forces (historical, economic, ethnic, religious, and so forth) do you see converging today?*

3. *How essential do you think the historical legacy is or should be in defining present identity?*

4. *How do you understand the role of Lutheran identity on your campus? What is/should be your role in maintaining it, in your opinion?*

5. *What challenges are there to maintaining church relatedness on your campus? Are there constructive ways to respond?*

3   The Theological Legacy

In addition to the historical influences discussed in the previous chapter, there also are specific theological concepts and doctrines that have informed the development of Lutheran higher education. While an exhaustive listing of these resources is beyond the scope of this book, seven of the major theological influences will be summarized briefly, followed by a consideration of three models of Christian higher education that come from the Protestant tradition.

For the reformers, theology to be legitimate must find embodiment in life, and so it is no accident that differing theological commitments came to inform differing educational approaches. A comparison of the Reformed and Anabaptist traditions in education will give a clearer picture of how the Lutheran tradition distinguishes itself from its other Protestant and Roman Catholic brethren. We begin, then, with a brief overview of the main theological themes of the Lutheran tradition before addressing how these themes give rise to a model for education.

I. THEOLOGICAL INFLUENCES

Theology is the "study of God" and in service to the church attempts to propose relations between the testimony of the community of faith (word) and the life of that community in nature and history (world).[1] Theology in the Lutheran tradition is confessional theology, which is both dynamic and dialectical, a specific witness in time and place to what is understood to be the central claim of the Christian faith. Lutheran theology, in effect, sings primarily one theme with variations, that of justification by grace through faith.

Justification by Faith

Luther's religious quest has been typified as the search for a righteous God, that is, one who would forgive for all eternity and not simply condemn the sinner out of hand. The forgiveness of sins is so central to Luther's thought and experience that one should not describe his theology as a string of doctrinal pearls strung one after another along the cord of justification, but rather as a blossoming flower (the Lutheran rose), the petals of which unfold from its center in justification. Until one can see the relationship of any doctrine to the forgiveness of sins, one has not fully understood Luther's thought. It is for this reason that

Luther formulated the four great *solas,* or "alones," of the Reformation—
Sola Gratia, "Grace Alone"; *Sola Scriptura,* "Scripture Alone"; *Sola Fide,*
"Faith Alone"; and *Solus Christus,* "Christ Alone." These four *solas* are
like the petals of the Lutheran rose radiating out affirming forgiveness of
sins by God's grace alone as recorded in the Scriptures alone and
embraced in faith alone, which trusts in Christ alone.

Following Luther, the Lutheran tradition is a confessional movement
in the church catholic, and this is its primary confession. It all centers on
justification by grace through faith (Romans 3:28), on God's gracious and
unmerited forgiveness on our behalf as incarnated in Christ and revealed
in Scripture. It is the doctrine by which the church stands or falls. The
Christian is then called to respond in faith understood as trust in the
promise and forgiveness of God. This leads to a life of grace-filled freedom and loving service, of joyful hope and commitment.

Saint Paul believed that such faith is also the basis for true community: "'For there is no distinction between Jew and Greek; the same Lord
is Lord of all and is generous to all who call on him'" (Romans 10:12).
This community also may include an academic community that reflects
upon the implications of justification by faith for life and understanding
in the world. The freedom of the gospel of God's justifying grace empowers faith for free and open inquiry, faith that seeks understanding.

The Doctrine of the Incarnation

The principle of the incarnation is that the spiritual is manifest in the
material, that the "Word became flesh" (John 1:14) so that *the finite does
contain the infinite.* This was the hallmark of Luther's theology, for out of
the incarnation flows God's justifying grace and forgiveness of sins. By
becoming creature, the Creator has sanctified human earthly existence,
reconciling us not only to God but also to one another and the earth.

Luther was a relational thinker. He saw all human life existing simultaneously in relationship with God and neighbor, so all human life, including the life of faith, is to be expressed through a dialectical understanding.
It is the simultaneity of these relationships that gives human life its tension
but also its ultimate meaning, and it is this dialectical relationship that is
established through the incarnation. The relationship before God is one
maintained by God's grace alone and trusted in by the Christian through
faith. According to Luther, the Christian relates to God through faith
alone, which is then expressed in loving service to one's neighbor. Such is
the freedom of a Christian when one is called upon to be a "little Christ" to
one's neighbor by continuing in limited human fashion the incarnation of

God's love in Christ. The incarnation thus not only reconciles the sinner to God, but it also provides the paradigm for Christian life and vocation.

Law and Gospel

In Luther's view the law has two functions in the earthly kingdom. First, it has a civil or ordering function in the world. Such orderliness is an expression of God's creation and prerequisite to the health of the earthly kingdom and its inhabitants. Civil law is the social expression of natural law found in the creation. All people are subject to these laws, whether Christian or not. A particular implication of this formulation was Luther's insistence that in the earthly kingdom the Christian is called to make common cause with all people, including those of other faiths, in providing for a just and healthy world. George W. Forell suggests that this understanding equips Lutherans with a distinctive insight and capacity for providing leadership and service in an increasingly multicultural world. This view allows, indeed requires, that believers transcend religious and political differences for the sake of the common good.[2]

Second, the law has a theological function—to convict of sin. By convicting us of our sin in the sight of God's will for all people, we come to see our need for forgiveness and are thus open to the saving grace of God, the good news of the gospel. As such, the theological use of the law also functions as a preparation for the gospel and thus exists in dialectical tension with it. To have the law without the gospel is to have judgment without hope, and to have the gospel without the law is not to count the cost of the cross, to have what Bonhoeffer calls "cheap grace." In response to this redeeming grace we accept the call to service, or vocation, in the earthly kingdom.

Christian Vocation

Luther's conviction concerning vocation was that the medieval church had too greatly separated church (the heavenly kingdom) and world (the earthly kingdom). The only worthy, holy callings at that time came to be understood as those whose work was associated with the heavenly kingdom—for example, those in religious orders and the clerical state that were set apart from the world. In contrast, Luther contended that all Christians are priests called by God to service in the earthly kingdom.[3] In Luther's view, since having received the gift of grace by faith, Christians respond to the call of God by serving their neighbors in the world. Thus all Christians become priests, and the calling to holy orders is not somehow superior to the calling of a street sweeper.

It is out of this paradigm of the two kingdoms that Lutherans have developed formulations on faith and learning, Christ and culture.[4] Motivated by grace and called by the gospel, Lutherans seek to understand the ways in which faith influences the academic calling. In part the paradigm places calling in the context of the divine eschaton (the end time) that gives meaning and direction to existence. In part the doctrine legitimizes the academic endeavor as a worthy secular undertaking, which, by its own standards and procedures, advances civilizing work in the world. This provides specific values and insights that enable Lutherans to envision and effect the academic calling in new ways.

Simultaneously Saint and Sinner

It was Luther's conviction that all people are both saint and sinner, *simul iustus et peccator.* In his doctrine of original sin Luther pointed out that humans are incapable of saving themselves, of purging every evil thought from their minds. All are prone to idolatry, the raising up of other gods in our lives. This notion was not original with Luther, but he and his colleagues gave particular expression to it. In Luther's words: "Both things are true; that I am righteous here with an incipient righteousness; and that in hope I am strengthened against sin and look for the consummation of perfect righteousness in heaven."[5]

In the academy this insight about human nature is often expressed in the Lutheran penchant for the paradoxical: Humans are both saint and sinner, see but only dimly and in part, are free yet bound, are in the world but not of the world, do not do the good that they would, and do the evil that they would not. As K. Glen Johnson observes, Lutherans seem to be "bears for punishment" with tension-filled distinctions such as law and gospel, faith and works, saint and sinner, finite and infinite, reason and faith.[6] According to Niebuhr, "in the polarity and tension of Christ and culture, life must be lived precariously and sinfully in the hope of a justification which lies beyond history."[7]

Lutherans have a penchant for "on the one hand, but on the other hand" types of argument. Perhaps this notion of simultaneously being saint and sinner explains in part a Lutheran bias for historical studies that often serve to cool ardor for quick solutions to complex problems and sharpen the debate on ethics in the academy and the public square. Perhaps it also explains why Lutherans are hesitant to jump on bandwagons—academic, religious, or political. At its best this notion staves off the perfectionist, triumphalist, City-of-God mentality. At its worst, it leads to quietism and inaction in that same arena.

Confessional Heritage

Faith finds its home in the church, the assembly of all believers called by the Word. The colleges were created and are partially sustained by the church. In this symbiosis (life together) the college primarily serves the church by preparing people for Christian vocation. As members of the church body, colleges provide regular occasions for worship and proclamation of the gospel, make provision for celebration of the sacraments, and support pastoral ministry and counsel to the community in Christian spirit.

Accordingly, the confessions of the church are fundamental to the identity and self-understanding of the church and her colleges. The Lutheran church sees itself in the Orthodox Christian tradition and affirms the central creeds of the church, including the Athanasian, Nicene, and Apostles' creeds. In addition, Lutherans give allegiance to the Augsburg Confession, the Smalcald Articles, and the Formula of Concord. [8] These statements provide both believers and scholars with useful paradigms for inquiry and self-understanding. In Lutheran fashion, such statements are human creations and subject to revision on the basis of yet new understandings of truth. The academic institutions of the church, colleges and seminaries, carry special responsibility in this regard as frontier places for the engagement of Word and world.

Ecumenical Commitment

A final shaping influence in the Lutheran tradition is the commitment to ecumenical (communal) dialogue. Luther was committed to the pursuit of truth in religious matters. His ninety-five theses were intended to provide a basis for debate, for joint inquiry. It was the tradition of Luther and his colleagues to debate vigorously with one another and engage in dialogue with other reformers. In the spirit of Luther, creeds, confessions, and doctrines are proximate visions of God's relationship to God's people, and, as such, they are subject to debate and reformulation. Indeed, Luther did not intend to form a separate denomination. At its best, Lutheranism is not to be understood as a denomination but rather as a confessional movement within the church catholic. It is a way of understanding the relationship between God and the world characterized by justifying grace embraced through faith.

As such a confessional movement, the way of Lutheranism contributes to ecumenical dialogue and also affects the way faith and learning are exemplified in institutions of higher learning. The character of Lutheran identity began, and must be sustained through, public debate and dialogue in the arena of contemporary intellectual and religious opinions. At their best, Lutheran scholars eagerly bring their tradition and confessions to the ecumenical table in the spirit of openness and commitment to the discernment of new truths about God and God's world. This is to say that "Lutheran liberal arts" is the arena in which the character of Lutheran identity was formulated and is to be sustained.

Taken together, these theological and confessional resources provide both content and context for the engagement of faith and learning, a dialogue that is explicit in the Lutheran educational mission. In faithfulness to the tradition, these materials do not provide an excuse for indoctrination but an occasion for dialogue. The tradition provides colleges with both the freedom and the responsibility to confront culture. Jesus moved about in the culture of his day. He addressed it directly and spoke in parables about it and God's wishes for it. Any dialogue that he initiated was creative and lively. On occasion he stirred up a hornet's nest, and on other occasions he calmed storms. Lutheran colleges are free, indeed obliged, to follow this example.

II. MODELS FOR CHRISTIAN HIGHER EDUCATION

One of the most helpful ways to understand the Lutheran tradition in higher education and its unique theological perspectives is to compare it with two of the other great branches of the Protestant Reformation and how they approach education.[9] Looking at how each of these traditions approaches the relation of faith and learning also will clarify the way they address education in general. While Lutherans represent one great wing of the Reformation, there are two others that have exerted considerable influence, that of the Reformed and Anabaptist traditions. For simplicity I will employ three prepositions to describe these traditions: "under" for the Reformed, "in" for the Anabaptist, and "with" for the Lutheran. Brief mention also will be made of the great Roman Catholic tradition in higher education, which may be characterized as "through." Let us turn first to the Reformed tradition.

The Reformed Tradition

At the heart of the Reformed tradition in education is the thought of John Calvin (1509–64). Central to Calvin's thought is the sovereignty of God over all creation. The Christian's task is to place all life and thought *under* God's sovereignty. Calvin attempted to create in Geneva a model city where every aspect of life was placed under God's sovereignty—its religion, art, politics, music, and social behavior. Since then, the same vision has motivated Calvinists to bring all aspects of life under God's sovereignty, including education. Religion scholar Richard Hughes observes, "Reformed educators seek to place the entire curriculum—and every course within the curriculum—under the sovereignty of God. According to this purpose all learning should be Christian in both purpose and orientation."[10]

In accordance with this approach the Reformed tradition employs four concepts to approach education. First, *all truth is God's truth,* so God is understood to be the author not only of faith but of every facet of life. Second, the goal of education is the *integration of faith and learning.* Hughes observes, "Because all truth is God's truth, secular learning and Christian faith can and should be integrated into a coherent understanding of reality."[11] This then leads to the third concept, that of a *Christian worldview.* What this implies, then, is that there is an integrated Christian perspective to every subject and discipline in the curriculum, and that anything outside the worldview has not been brought under the sovereignty of God and must be so integrated. Finally, *secularization* is a problem for the Reformed tradition because it means that something—some discipline, experience, concept, and so forth—has not been brought under God's sovereignty and stands as a challenge to that worldview. As Hughes observes, "Because the possibility of secularization is so real in this context, the notion of a *slippery slope* is a metaphor that many in this tradition take very seriously."[12] Anything not under the Christian worldview, and thus not under the sovereignty of God, stands as a challenge to the assumption that all truth is God's truth and therefore to the integration of faith and learning. Clearly the word "under" is the dominate relationship in the Reformed tradition.

Given all its intellectual power and commitment, there are two dangers in this position—triumphalism and distortion.[13] There is the strong pressure to fit or subsume all disciplines and issues under the Christian worldview, to see it as intellectually superior and "triumphant" over all others. This can lead to the distortion of material and to a form of doctrinal imposition that sees the Christian perspective as the final and only viable one, thus denying any genuine pluralism and the opportunity for dialogue. Does the integrity of the academic enterprise suffer when all knowledge has to be brought under the hegemony of one worldview? It can, though it need not.

Clearly this is a powerful Christian expression in higher education, and some of the greatest thinkers on the subject are to be found in this tradition—people such as Arthur Holmes, Mark Noll, Nicholas Wolterstorff,

Nathan Hatch, George Marsden, and Richard Mauw. An impressive list indeed! They represent one of the most conscientious intellectual attempts to integrate modern intellectual concerns with the Christian faith. It is a top-down enterprise with considerable philosophical rigor and a clearly articulated position that many find very appealing and marketable. Given the prolific production of scholars in this tradition, one could be led to think that this is the only Christian option in higher education today, but it is not. Now let's turn to an example from the Anabaptist perspective—the Mennonite tradition.

The Mennonite Tradition

While the Reformed tradition approaches education from a Christian worldview perspective and attempts to place all life *under* God's sovereignty and reconcile all knowledge with Christian doctrine, the Mennonite tradition takes the opposite approach, from *in* the world, and makes connection through loving service to the neighbor. Their call is to radical discipleship.[14] The role of doctrine is very limited in this tradition. Instead, the role of communal, self-sacrificial service is their hallmark. Taking their name from the reformer Menno Simons (1496–1561), who broke with the Roman Catholic church in 1536, they emphasize believer baptism and congregational responsibility, deny any church hierarchy, and stress nonresistance.[15]

One of the Mennonite colleges, Goshen College, pioneered service-learning programs in the developing world. Clearly this tradition understands that education takes place through communal service and encounter with other traditions, peoples, and experiences. There is not a great concern for doctrinal, intellectual integration, but one for loving witness through service. As one of the most well-known "peace" churches, the Mennonite tradition understands what radical witness might involve and that nonresistance has not been the majority expression in Christian history. Yet they are willing to make the sacrifices necessary to affirm their witness to what they understand to be the radical character of Jesus' message. This very radical call, however, also can be a liability if it separates one community from another or leads to a narrowness and exclusivity by involving only those who are able to embrace the radical call.

We have then two very historic and different approaches to Christian higher education in these traditions. Richard Hughes sums up the difference quite nicely in quoting from a Mennonite scholar he interviewed at Goshen College: "The Reformed model, she observed, tends to be cerebral and therefore transforms living by thinking. The Mennonite model, on the other hand, transforms thinking by living and by one's commitment to a radically Christocentric lifestyle. For this reason, she suggested, the Reformed model may be particularly suitable to graduate education, while the Mennonite model may be especially appropriate for undergraduate learning."[16]

The Lutheran Tradition

Between these two positions of intellectual worldview and radical service there is a third position, which, I believe, is typified by the Lutheran tradition. The Lutheran tradition, based on the principal of justification by grace through faith, is characterized by paradox, by the dialectical tension between the finite and the infinite in the world and the ambiguous nature of that world and human life. Rather than resolving to either the intellect or service, the Lutheran tradition attempts to keep them in simultaneous tension with one another. The word typifying the Lutheran tradition is "with." God is *with us* in the incarnation and throughout our daily lives. It is this "withness," this *"simul"* or simultaneity, that leads to mutual affirmations in tension.

Luther certainly argued for God's sovereignty, but this constantly has to be kept in relationship to human finitude. God's sovereignty does not mean it must be imposed on an unbelieving world, as Calvin attempted in Geneva, but that the human is not God and that therefore all our capacities—intellectual, physical, moral—also are finite and thereby incomplete and fragmentary. As Richard Hughes observes, "The sovereignty of God means that I am not God, that my reason is inevitably impaired, and that my knowledge is always fragmentary and incomplete. In the context of higher education and the life of the mind, this position means that every scholar must always confess that he or she could be wrong."[17]

This means then that doubt is the partner of faith since in the midst of a finite world all knowing and believing is undertaken by a finite mind and heart. All our knowing of the infinite and the divine is through the finite, that is, through masks of God that open to the divine but never fully disclose it. This means then, that a sharp line between the sacred and the secular cannot be drawn for the Lutheran tradition. All of the finite world can in some way become a mask for God and therefore must be kept in constant relationship with faith. This is the source of the dialectic, the paradox of faith, for Luther.

Paradox stands at the heart of the Lutheran tradition precisely because Luther refused to separate the life of faith from life in the world.

Luther insisted on the Christian life being lived right in the midst of the world. The resources of faith must be brought into play in daily work and life instead of in some separated, ostensibly more holy or religious sphere such as a monastery. This simultaneity is affirmed in the Lutheran understanding of *simul justus et peccator,* or "at the same time justified and sinner." We remain sinful in the world even though at the same time, through faith in God's grace, we are justified and accepted by God. This gives rise to the two kingdoms or realms of Luther's thought—the world of today (the natural world), governed by law, and the world to come (the kingdom of God), governed by grace. The Christian lives in the interface or the overlap by being in the world but not of the world. The Christian lives in both worlds, those of nature and of grace, simultaneously. Richard Hughes summarizes:

> The authentic Lutheran vision, therefore, never calls for Lutherans to superimpose the kingdom of God on the world as the Reformed tradition seeks to do. Nor does it call for Lutherans to separate from the world as the heirs of the Anabaptists often seek to do. Instead, the Christian must reside in two worlds at one and the same time: the world of nature and of grace. The Christian in Luther's view, therefore, is free to take seriously *both* the world *and* the Kingdom of God.[18]

This dynamic "withness" sustains dialogue and does not fear a slippery slope into secularity. Rather, it is all of life, including that which is labeled secular, for it too is part of God's creation that must be brought into dynamic relationship with faith and the potentially transforming grace of God. It is this very dynamic that sustains openness and academic freedom in higher education, while at the same time insisting on bringing this world of knowledge into dynamic relationship with the Christian faith. The result often can be messy, paradoxical, and ambiguous, but that is where faith gives one the strength to continue on. Life need not be simple and clear to be livable or intelligible. Hughes observes, "The task of the Christian scholar, therefore, is not to impose on the world—or on the material that he or she studies—a distinctly 'Christian worldview.' Rather, the Christian scholar's task is to study the world as it is and then to bring that world into dialogue with the Christian vision of redemption and grace."[19] This model results in dialogue rather than in imposition.

There is, of course, a danger in this paradoxical or simultaneous view—namely that one can collapse the tension to one side or the other. One can collapse into a form of dogmatic absolutism that does not recognize the integrity of the other, to accentuate the kingdom of God at the expense of the everyday world. Or one can go full speed into the everyday and collapse into some form of radical pluralism or thoroughgoing relativism. The dangers of legalism have been present in Lutheran history, and the temptation to relativism always dogs contemporary thought. If the "withness" is affirmed and the simultaneity is not allowed to collapse, then the Lutheran tradition can be a creative catalyst for the ongoing engagement of the Christian tradition with contemporary life and thought in a way that differs from the other great models of the Protestant tradition. Clearly each model has its strengths and weaknesses, and the goal is to maintain the vitality of all the models so they each can contribute their own unique perspective to Christian higher education.

A brief mention also must be made of the other great Christian tradition in higher education in this country, that of the Roman Catholic church. Here the incarnational and sacramental vision of the Christian life clearly holds sway, and there is no strong aversion to the secular. In this regard the Roman Catholic view would be closer to the Lutheran. But there also are Roman Catholic institutions that make a radical call to discipleship the heart of their programs and are thus closer to the Mennonite tradition.

There is considerable variety within the Roman Catholic tradition due principally to the different religious orders that have established the various schools. There is the historic Benedictine commitment to community and hospitality and the Jesuit use of Thomism and natural law, for example. Such diversity makes it difficult to speak of a stereotypical Roman Catholic school. If there is one word to describe the Roman Catholic vision of higher education, it would be "through." Through the creation, God is mediating blessing and grace but also calling the Christian into radical service to and for the world.

Thus we can talk about models of Christian higher education that seek to put everything "under" God's sovereign rule in an integrating Christian worldview. We also can talk about models based on radical discipleship "in" the world, which stress service over intellectual construction. We can talk of a model of simultaneity and paradox, a model that attempts to talk at the same time both about the world and about faith, of nature "with" grace. We also can see Christian witness and service involved "through" life in the world. Each of these models and a number of others may well be found on our college campuses. Each of the models discussed has a long and rich history replete with an integrity all its own.

For Lutheran institutions, the Lutheran model holds the most promise and needs to find embodiment on our campuses. This commitment does *not,* however, mean to exclude other models embodied by different faculty from their respective traditions. In the challenging years ahead, Christian higher education is going to need all the resources it can muster in addressing the needs of a rapidly changing global society. Certainly within the Lutheran model there is room for other voices and models to find expression as we seek the common goal of instruction in the faith and in the world.

QUESTIONS FOR REFLECTION

1. *What excites you about your field/discipline and opens up the mysteries of life for you?*

2. *What elicits wonder and awe from you in your field? Can it be seen as a "mask" of the transcendent?*

3. *How does or can theology connect with your discipline? Does the Lutheran paradoxical approach help? Should it?*

4. *Do you think secularization is a problem for Christian higher education? Why or why not?*

5. *Which model of Christian higher education do you find most attractive? Why? Which do you think are found on your campus?*

6. *How essential is the theological legacy in defining the present identity of your institution?*

4   Christian Vocation in the Liberal Arts

We have seen that throughout its history the Lutheran tradition has placed a strong emphasis upon education—first of all for the preparation of clergy and then for political leaders and the general population.[1] This emphasis came from Luther's understanding that the Christian is to be actively involved in the world and, by so doing, exercise his or her Christian vocation as a way of being a co-creator with God in sustaining the creation itself. In later Lutheranism, however, a duality developed between faith and life such that vocation became primarily identified with one's occupation (Lutheran orthodoxy) or with personal piety (Lutheran pietism). It is not so much that these interpretations were wrong as that they were incomplete.[2]

These changes, along with other forces such as the Enlightenment, helped to create the more secular understanding of vocation that we find in the twentieth century. This in turn directly has affected liberal-arts study because in more recent years there has developed a strong emphasis upon career and job preparation on the part of undergraduate students. While this is understandable, it has, because of a separation from its theological roots in the doctrine of vocation, made liberal-arts study less significant and led to the unnecessary separation of one's religious convictions from one's life in the workaday world. Indeed it even has led to seeing college itself as a "holding pattern" away from the "real world" where people will begin to exercise their opportunities and responsibilities.

The thesis of this chapter is that scholarship itself is a spiritual endeavor and therefore is an acceptable expression of Christian vocation. Such an understanding of scholarship can help our students to correct the occupationalism of our time and strengthen the value of liberal-arts education. In light of this vocational understanding of scholarship, it will be argued that students are exercising their Christian vocation while studying in an undergraduate liberal-arts context and that this is a valid expression of their vocation apart from whatever particular callings they pursue upon graduation. It is hoped that this brief chapter not only will show the value of Christian vocation for understanding liberal-arts study, but also affirm this vocation on the part of both faculty and students in undergraduate liberal-arts education.

Clearly there is much that could be said concerning the understanding of vocation from the perspective of many different disciplines, and I will make no attempt to be exhaustive. Rather, I will highlight some of the historical and theological issues that I believe help in understanding where we have come from and where this might lead us. By focusing upon Luther's understanding of vocation, I do not assume that he has the final word on all matters; certainly, some necessary changes must be made between his time and ours. His work forms the basis of this book because Lutheran colleges are a part of this historical tradition and Lutheranism has made significant contributions to higher education in general.

There are many issues facing undergraduate liberal-arts education, and this chapter focuses on only one of them, namely the issue of "occupationalism." (We shall look at several others in succeeding chapters.) In light of this focus, the chapter will be divided into three sections: "Luther on Christian Vocation," "Scholarship as a Spiritual Endeavor," and "Christian Vocation in the Liberal Arts." It is hoped that a broad consideration of the Christian understanding of vocation can provide a framework not only to confront the dualistic thinking of many of our students but also to place their scholarly work in a more inclusive and edifying context.

I. LUTHER ON CHRISTIAN VOCATION

Before turning to a discussion of Luther's concept of Christian vocation, it would be helpful to review briefly the biblical understanding of this concept. In the biblical witness the primary word used to express vocation is the word meaning "to call,"[3] which is explicitly associated with a call from God. The calling of God always proceeds from God's grace and is an invitation to participate in the blessings of God's creation through that same grace. It is not a call out of the world but into it, and, especially in the Hebrew Scriptures, it is corporate.[4] Indeed, in the Hebraic understanding, the fundamental purpose of human creation is to give glory to God, humanity's creator, and this is done principally in this life. God's purpose in the creation is shalom, which is peace incarnated in love through justice, a love providing all that is necessary for life.

Understanding God's activity as such, theologian Dorothy Soelle observes, "Whatever meaning we find in the concept of creation, in a creator, and in our having been created hinges on love. The concept of creation is rendered empty and meaningless if it is not out of love that God created the world."[5] This creation out of love then elicits a loving response on the part of the creatures created out of love. Thus one can view the calling from God ultimately to be the reciprocation of God's love in the world through human imaging of that love. If we are created in the image of God and God is love and the nature of creation is a work of love, then we are called to embody love in our work in the world. Work is not punishment; it is service on behalf of the Creator.

One of the direct consequences of love, of course, is justice. Justice is the proximate embodiment of love in society. As Soelle reminds us, our works of love in the world also must be works of justice and liberation.[6] Thus the call of God touches all that we do in life, especially our work. This concept of call then places all earthly human endeavor in a theological, or transcendent, context in light of which it derives its ultimate significance. It is precisely the loss of this context that threatens us today, changing an incarnational notion of vocation based upon the call of God into primarily a carnal one based on material satisfaction.

In the New Testament the complete embodiment of this biblical vision of vocation is found in the person of Jesus Christ. Jesus was called by God and fulfills the promises of God upon which the understanding of vocation rests. As chapter one of the book of Genesis relates, the whole creation is voiced forth from the word of God, and St. John (1:1-14) records that this word, this *logos,* is one with God and is God and has entered *into* human flesh. This is to say that the second person of the Trinity, the *logos,* was the means for the creation. This means of creation within God then, through the incarnation, enters into the creation that it has made possible. The Creator becomes one with the creation. The principle impelling both creation and incarnation is the divine love of God so that all existence is a symbiosis, a life together, in love proceeding from the love of creation and reconciled and restored through the incarnation of that love in Jesus Christ. Such was Jesus' calling, and the Christian calling then follows upon this symbiosis.

The Christian is called (*klesis,* as Paul uses the term—see Romans 8:30 and 1 Corinthians 7:20) then to trust in this promise of God through faith and live out this faith through loving service to one's neighbor in the world. As this understanding of the Christian call developed through the centuries, particularly with the rise of the monastic movements, it became increasingly identified with specific "religious" callings. One sees this in Augustine's *Confessions,* where to follow one's Christian calling is to seek "Christian perfection,"[7] a pursuit not available to the ordinary person, for one had to leave "worldly" occupations to pursue it. Church historian Constance Gengenbach observes, "By the latter Middle Ages the very words *vocatio* and *Ruf* meant the official calling of a candidate to a clerical benefice by those who had power of ecclesiastical appointment. Christian vocation was thus split off from the ordinary life of human beings in the world."[8]

It was this separation of the Christian calling from the world that Martin Luther and the Reformation were to change radically. It may be that Luther's particular contribution in the understanding of the Christian calling was to connect it specifically to one's station or work in life.[9] In a very real sense the Reformation, by emphasizing the priesthood of all believers and denying any superiority to specifically "religious" vocations, brought about a secularization of the understanding of vocation and, by so doing, returned it to its original biblical roots.

One of the primary bases for the understanding of the Christian calling and vocation is the role of hope—the impact of the transcendent future upon present action. It is this emphasis that Luther explicitly develops in his understanding of the two rules or kingdoms of God. Luther was a relational thinker. He saw all human life as existing simultaneously in relationship with God and neighbor, so all discussion of human life, including the life of faith, is to be expressed through a dialectical understanding. It is the simultaneity of these relationships that gives human life its tension but also its ultimate meaning. The relationship before God (*coram Deo*) is one maintained by God's grace alone and trusted in by the Christian through faith, the ground for hope. According to Luther, the Christian relates to God though faith alone (*sola fide*). That is not the end of the relationships, however, for the Christian also lives in the worlds of nature and history, so there is a relationship to the world (*coram mundo*) that is maintained in love, the ground for present action.

According to Luther, one relates to God through faith and to one's neighbor through love.[10] What this means then is that vocation belongs exclusively to *this* world. For Luther, we do not exercise our vocation in order to please God or gain entrance into the world to come, but rather, following the Hebraic emphasis, vocation is for this life and done primarily for the neighbor.[11] This is where the understanding of the two kingdoms enters in. In the kingdom of the world to come (God's future kingdom and the ground for Christian hope), God rules directly through the gospel, and the law does not function, for it has been fulfilled. The Christian in the world of today lives in anticipation of this kingdom while living in this world as a justified sinner. This future kingdom overlaps with the world of today precisely in the lives of individual Christians. For Luther, there is nothing that particularly distinguishes Christians from non-Christians in regard to life in the present world. All stand under the command and judgment of the law, in both its civil use (the first use) to maintain order in society and its theological use (the second use) to convict of sin.

It is particularly in relation to the first use of the law that Luther understands the role of Christian vocation in the world of today. The first use of the law is grounded in the order of creation itself, whereby there is a creation rather than a chaos. The biblical understanding of this order in creation is that God continues to maintain the creation, even uphold it, in the face of chaos. Creation is understood to be ongoing (*creatio continua*) and not a once-and-for-all occurrence that is over and done. Drawing upon this understanding, Luther sees the first use of the law as grounding "stations" or "offices" in society in which humans can participate with God in continuing the creation. One of the functions of being created in God's image is that humans become co-creators with God in sustaining the creation itself.

Christian vocation then follows the demands of the law, both natural and civil, in maintaining nature and society. Here is where the Christian's calling to loving service is expressed. Vocation for Luther, as Swedish theologian Gustaf Wingren brings out, is more then just one's occupation; it entails all that one does in the world. Vocation includes personal, communal, and historical relationships as well as occupational.[12] Luther Seminary Dean Marc Kolden summarizes this understanding concisely when he states:

> Vocation belongs to our situation between baptism and the final resurrection—a situation in which there are two kingdoms (earth and heaven, in Luther's terminology), two contending powers (God and the devil), two antagonistic components within the Christian person (the old self and the new self), and when Christians are involved in constant struggle. Vocation is our calling in our situation in life, through which we serve God's creative work being under the law.[13]

The world of today is not a neutral place; rather, it is one of competing and conflicting powers in which struggle is a daily experience. It is for this reason that Luther argued against leaving the world for the cloister, for this would be to abdicate one's calling to serve God against the forces of destruction present in the world. Vocation is for the earth and the world of today so that, as Wingren summarizes, "Human action is a medium for God's love to others."[14] Luther had a dialectical rather than dualistic conception of Christian life. It is this dialectical movement that allowed him to see the action of God in the world even when this action was hidden behind the "masks" (*larvae*) of God in creation. This dialectical tension allows the Christian to live in *both* the world of today and the world to come as well as to immerse herself or himself in the life of this world through Christian freedom. Such is the power of faith in life.

The tragedy of later Lutheranism is that it became uncomfortable with this dialectical tension and collapsed it into a dualism that saw vocation as personal spirituality and left the public sphere to the devil or secular authority alone (which at times in Western history has amounted to the same thing). In Lutheran orthodoxy this dualism led to political quietism that did not see as necessary a prophetic voice to be uttered in the area of public policy or social matters. Later pietism, on the other hand, turned inward to a personal understanding of the call that saw it primarily in relationship to God and not to neighbor. H. Richard Niebuhr summarizes this condition:

> Luther's answer to the Christ-and-culture question was that of a dynamic, dialectical thinker. Its reproductions by many who called themselves his followers were static and undialectical. They substituted two parallel moralities for his closely related ethics. As faith became a matter of belief rather than a fundamental, trustful orientation of the person in every moment toward God, so the freedom of the Christian man became autonomy in all the spheres of culture. It is a great error to confuse this parallelistic dualism of separated spiritual and temporal life with the interactionism of Luther's gospel of faith in Christ working by love in the world of culture.[15]

This parallelistic dualism permitted the separation of religious reflection from society and only was intensified by the intellectual developments of the Enlightenment and, later, natural as well as social scientific thought. Other branches of the Reformation, such as Calvinism, did not suffer the dualistic fate that Lutheranism courted but rather succumbed to an equally dangerous collapse of the separation of the two kingdoms into an implied identification of religious election with success or failure in this world. It was not Lutheran dualism but the opposite stance in Calvinism that was responsible for the final conversion of work as a Christian vocation into work as worldly success.[16]

Neither Luther nor Calvin would have supported the later developments made from their thought, but this history of transformation has brought us to the present day, when vocation has become synonymous with occupation and the primary value of occupations is defined in financial terms. It is this condition that is now so perniciously intruding into undergraduate liberal-arts education, seeing it primarily as glorified technical training to get the "better" jobs and not seeing it as preparation for life itself and ongoing contributions of service to one's neighbor. Scholarship then becomes seen as a technical endeavor rather than a spiritual activity giving glory to God. One of the tasks of Christian liberal-arts study is to retrieve this spiritual understanding.

II. SCHOLARSHIP AS A SPIRITUAL ENDEAVOR

The principle of the incarnation is that the spiritual is manifest in the material. Just as the divine and human natures of Christ are found to be indissoluble and indistinguishable, so too the understanding of the human coming from the Hebraic heritage of the Christian tradition emphasizes human existence as a somatopsychic unity, a unity of body and soul. The spiritual is not understood as "other worldly" or necessarily "supernatural" but rather as concretely involved in physical existence in this life. The root meaning of "spirit" in the Hebrew Scriptures is "wind" or "breath" (*ruach*), which animates life and moves all of creation. By extension it became the life principle and also is associated with God as life giver and human beings as those created in the image of God.[17] This is one of the consequences of the doctrine of creation and its innate goodness, of which human creaturehood is a part.

The spiritual dimensions of life for Luther, following this Hebraic heritage, are to be expressed in this life with the mindfulness of a life to come. Christian theology formally denies a soul/body dualism as found in classical Greek philosophy, emphasizing rather the resurrection of the body. Whatever eternal life is to be like, it is not a disembodied existence, but it must find some form of physical expression as well, hence St. Paul's reference to "spiritual bodies" in 1 Corinthians 15:44-50.[18] As discussed in Chapter 1, spirituality is self-transcending selfhood that finds expression precisely in and through material, daily life. It is the means by which one transcends self-interest in order to be concerned about the neighbor. Fundamentally, the spiritual finds expression through faith and love in this life and embraces the simultaneous relationships discussed in the first part of this chapter. *To live out the spiritual character of one's life, then, is to live in faithful trust of God while expressing that faith in loving service to one's neighbor.*

This also is understood as a communal activity within the Christian tradition because the church exists in the world as the body of Christ. This body is animated and enlivened by the spirit of God and is the third person of the Trinity. It is the continuation of the "symbiosis of love" discussed earlier, by which the love of God not only voices forth the creation and incarnates for redemption but also permeates life for sanctification, calling all things closer to God in Christ. (The Holy Spirit "calls," "gathers," "enlightens," and "sanctifies," as Luther's Small Catechism puts it.) It is this theological framework within which Christian liberal-arts study is placed and in light of which scholarship itself can be seen as a spiritual endeavor.

The words "scholar" and "scholarship" both derive from the Latin word *schola,* which means "school." The word "scholastic" comes from the Greek *scholastikos,* which means "to keep a school" and is often associated with the scholastic schoolmen of the Middle Ages.[19] Study, as it was understood within the Christian context of the Middle Ages when the institution of the university was born, was seen as exercising one's God-given powers of reason and faith to study the works of God in creation. Indeed it was the unity of God's activity in creation that made the universe one, a "uni-" rather than a "multi-" verse, and which unified the "uni"-versity itself.

The study of the liberal arts, which began with the Greeks, chiefly with the Sophists,[20] by the Middle Ages was seen in the theological context of God's creation as one of the main ways in which to glorify God. Precisely because the liberal arts study life in all its diversity and the human in particular, their study can be seen as a spiritual activity. In their study, the living thought of the human spirit actively is engaged in contemplation of the life of creation itself and ultimately that of its Creator.

By the time of the Reformation, education was seen as an office in creation, which itself was created by God. On the basis of his work as a biblical expositor, Luther came to the conclusion that education was commanded by God.[21] It was seen as an extension of the family, which is one of the basic orders of creation, by means of which God seeks to sustain the creation itself. Thus the school, and the scholarship which follows from it, is seen as part of the earthly kingdom and exists for service in this world. Education and scholarly study are a legitimate expression of one's vocation, particularly when understood within the context of creation and done in loving service to one's neighbor. Christian vocation legitimately can be expressed through education, and scholarship and need not be seen as simply a means to some other end. Education and scholarship have their own religious integrity, and because they are to be exercised in this world, the arts and sciences would have their own integrity as well.

There is no need to "spiritualize" or "Christianize" the study of a particular discipline in order to make it acceptable to the Christian vision. (Contrast this with the Reformed model of Christian higher education discussed in the last chapter.) That is part of the power of Luther's dialectical understanding of the two kingdoms. Each realm has its own integrity, and within the realm of the world of today, the earthly kingdom, reason can reign supreme as a gift of God and an expression of the human spirit. As theologian David Lotz points out, "The truth is that no one praised reason more unstintingly than Luther insofar as reason does not claim competence in divine as well as human matters, but limits itself to its own domain. Within its own proper sphere—which is the realm of temporal government and human justice, of social, political, and economic arrangements, of humanistic education, culture, and civilization— reason is God's greatest gift and should rule as queen."[22]

Since this use of reason is conducted in the earthly realm, it can be conducted with freedom, for even the human will is not bound in relation to the world, only in relation to God. Lotz remarks, "The earthly kingdom—where reason rules and education finds its unqualified legitimation—is also the realm of human freedom. ... Education is itself an instrument and expression of this freedom of will, and exists to instruct the will to choose rightly and wisely."[23] This education is for service in the world, and both Luther and Melanchthon highly valued classical learning in the shaping of sound political and ethical judgments in worldly affairs. It follows, then, that academic freedom is essential to the pursuit of one's scholarly vocation because all fields have their own integrity and, as long as they remain in their respective spheres of study, should not be interfered with by theological or any other ideological perspectives.[24]

In light of this understanding of education as an expression of an office in creation and a legitimate expression of Christian vocation, it now is possible to pursue more directly discussion of scholarship as a spiritual endeavor. Scholarship becomes a spiritual activity precisely when it serves the needs of one's neighbor. As mentioned earlier, the principle of the incarnation sees the spiritual as manifest in the material, so people need not isolate themselves from the world in order to engage in spiritual activity. This isolation is a false understanding based on a dualistic rather than dialectical understanding of the two kingdoms. The spiritual permeates all of life in the world because theologically everything exists in the presence of God. There is no place where the spiritual has to be made present or where it is inappropriate to be found. In scholarly study one is engaged in spiritual activity by reflecting on creation, and therefore works in the presence of God.

The spiritual dimension of scholarship also enters through the spirituality of the scholar. By viewing his or her study in the presence of God's law, the scholar is engaged in spiritual activity. Such study is done mindful of the presence of God and is employed in service to one's neighbor by bringing added understanding to students or increased knowledge to the world.

Scholarship, then, can be a spiritual endeavor done in faith and loving service. When so performed, it is a legitimate expression of one's Christian vocation. The challenge in our final section is to see how this understanding of scholarship and vocation can be useful in addressing the false "occupationalism" of our time, particularly as it finds expression in undergraduate liberal-arts education.

III. CHRISTIAN VOCATION IN THE LIBERAL ARTS

The purpose of liberal-arts study is the study of the human in all its diversity and contexts. This is the *artes liberales* vision of education, which in the West harkens back to Isocrates and was given further definition by Cicero and Quintilian.[25] Its purpose was to train a good citizen or leader by teaching the skills of grammar, rhetoric, and logic, what became known as the *trivium,* which was supplemented in late antiquity by arithmetic, geometry, music, and astronomy, known as the *quadrivium.*[26]

For Christian liberal-arts study, the arts and sciences were affirmed and supplemented by theology. The fundamental context that provides unity to their study is the theological (see both Narum and Quanbeck's articles). Indeed it is the commitment to God as creator that permits the affirmation of the cosmos itself as a united cosmos, a universe. In light of this orientation, all studies of humanity and nature are seen as valid in their own right, with their own inherent dignity and integrity.

Today we face a number of challenges in undergraduate liberal-arts study. This chapter focuses on only one, that of "occupationalism," which seems to undermine the integrity and classical purpose of liberal-arts education. In light of our brief study of the Christian doctrine of vocation, at least three possible responses to this contemporary condition can be formulated: the need to deal with the dualistic stage of faith and psychological development that most college undergraduates enter with, the need to show the value of incarnational theology for connecting faith and learning, and the need to show the importance, within Christian education, of seeing all study in the context of the governance of God (theonomously). Let us turn briefly to each of these by way of concluding our discussion.

According to much recent research on college-aged students and work coming out of adult psychological development, most students around eighteen to twenty years of age are in a dualistic mind-set (see the work of William Perry in psychology, as well as James Fowler and Sharon Parks in faith development, the subject of the next chapter). This, of course, means that what students want from their instructors are the "right" answers. There is no sensitivity to context—historical, cultural, or otherwise—and this dualism carries over to their understanding of faith. One is right and the others are wrong since there is one true and correct position for everything.

Given this mind-set and the dualistic understanding of Christian vocation that many students receive from their home contexts, there is little wonder that they see no connection between faith and their choice of career, major, and so forth. When faith is seen primarily as a personal, private matter, separated from the public realm—the realm of work— then it has little bearing on the understanding of one's vocation, and vocation is reduced to the equivalent of an occupation. Within the Lutheran framework, this is a direct result of the inability of the tradition to keep in dialectical tension the two-kingdoms doctrine that Luther formulated. It collapses into a dualism either of private piety or occupationalism, and our students, given the material pressures of our society, have little with which to resist such a separation. Religious matters and values become private, personal, and therefore disposable in relation to the realm of work and material success.

One way to respond to this condition is to try to open up for our dualistic students a dialectical way of thinking that can hold positions in tension without necessarily reducing them to one side or the other. The problem is not with a secularized sense of vocation but *with only* a secularized sense, that is, a nondialectical one that does not relate vocation to the tension with faith and hope. It is hope, and the role of the transcendent future grounded in this hope, that can stand in critique over the present. It is in light of what *might be* that one is empowered to change *what is.*

This, of course, will take time and maturation on the students' part, but the point is we do them little service in either their vocational or faith understanding if we simply repeat back to them the dualistic answers they seek. Christian vocation as Luther envisioned it lives within the tensions of life. Faith is necessary precisely because the ways of God are not necessarily perceptible except under masks, which always opens up an element of doubt and uncertainty. Faith gives one the freedom to study this world in the midst of one's doubts and uncertainties. A more complete understanding of Christian vocation would permit the relating of faith and career in a dialectical fashion, as all faith is related to life. This, in turn, would begin to provide a basis for transcendent critique of the values of our society and one's place within it. Indeed this is part of the value of incarnational theology.

When one has a dualistic framework between faith and life situations, it is very difficult to see any of one's ordinary actions as spiritual. The spiritual becomes the exceptional, the mountaintop experiences, and the rest is just drab old work-a-day flesh. The principle of the incarnation, that the spiritual is manifest in the material, stands in direct contradiction to this type of spiritual dualism or separation. The spirit is the animating reality of life itself and, as such in biblical thought, could not be separated from the physical. It was what moved the physical.

The second task, then, is to assist our students in seeing themselves as spiritual beings, not disembodied spirits or despiritualized bodies.[27] It is to demonstrate how incarnational theology assists in overcoming dualism and connecting faith and learning. Spirituality must be embodied. This means bringing spirituality back down to earth, where it belongs in the first place. While students certainly still may see prayer and worship as spiritual activity, they also need to come to see their studies, their dates, their games, indeed all life's activities, as having a spiritual character. The spiritual means to express one's faith in loving service to one's neighbor, proceeding from the love of God experienced in grace for oneself. Spirituality consists in self-transcending selfhood connected with the life of the body and the material world.

Scholarship (learning) can be understood as a spiritual endeavor precisely because it is self-transcending in service to neighbor. It is an expression of one's vocation because it proceeds from one of the offices of society in service to the creation itself. We need to assist our students in seeing their studies incarnationally rather than carnally. This spiritual character of life opens up when one begins to see all that one does under the direction of God's care and guidance—to see beyond the immediately present in a more holistic and inclusive way, in light of God's activity in creation itself. This is not to see things in a fuzzy or weak-headed way, but rather it is to see the horizons of meaning that are present in every occasion of life. It is not out of life, but it places the occurrences of life in a wider context of meaning. It is to see more holistically to connect faith and learning.

Finally, this concern for holism helps us to see theonomously, to see everything under the care and governance of God. Since the time of Aristotle, the West has been impressed with the value and power of reductive analysis. To break a whole down into its constituent parts and to classify them was seen to be "knowing" what that whole was. This tradition became codified in natural science from the time of the Renaissance and still is with us today. More recently, an additional movement of holism has developed to help balance the reductive influences of analysis. It does not disallow the value of the part but seeks to see the whole as well. The whole is more than the sum of its parts, and one needs to deal with wholes as wholes. Holism focuses on the interconnections between elements in physical existence, particularly seeing their interdependence. This has given rise to an awareness of symbiosis on a global scale, and theologically it can be seen as based upon the symbiosis of God's love in creation itself. All life exists in interdependence precisely because it is a product of divine love, a symbiosis of love.

The environmental crisis was one of the first issues to raise the need for holism. It is not accidental that the environmental movement arose shortly after the first lunar landing. Space exploration has allowed us to see the earth as a totality. Scientist Frank White calls this the "Overview Effect," which gives us a more inclusive perspective upon ourselves.[28] Perhaps this experience is not dissimilar from that of the earlier age of exploration and how it redefined the place of Europe in the world.

The point is that this holism, deriving from a global perspective and done in faith, can be seen as one of the direct results of viewing one's life and studies in the context of God's care of creation. What one studies are the "laws" God has placed in the world, indeed the cosmos, by which unity and wholeness is possible and through which there is a creation rather than a chaos. This does not mean that one will verify divine governance in the physics lab; that is to confuse the two kingdoms again. Physics, as with all disciplines, has its own integrity, but there is the need for greater networking, for a more inclusive, holistic perspective in light of which these occurrences in physics can find meaning even beyond the discipline of physics. Traditionally this is known as a metaphysic or a worldview, what Neil Postman has referred to as a "mega-narrative" (see Chapter 1).

Part of the mission of a Christian liberal-arts college is to bring Christian faith reflection and worldview analysis into relationship with all the disciplines on campus. (See the Lutheran model of Christian higher education discussed in Chapter 3.) It is partly the freedom of the Christian faith that makes the liberal arts "liberating," for it assists that process of opening horizons of meaning and understanding by providing a ground or vision from which they can be related.

In the final analysis, what has been described under the concept of Christian vocation is nothing less than the practice of spiritual formation. Such formation includes the integration of the spiritual and the material, the overcoming of false dualisms that separate faith from learning, and the cultivation of a more inclusive perspective grounded in the unity of the Creator with the creation itself. A more careful consideration of the Christian understanding of vocation within the liberal-arts context would assist such spiritual formation.

QUESTIONS FOR REFLECTION

1. *How do you balance the understanding of service to others with the drive for self-advancement?*

2. *Does vocation seem to be a corrective to occupationalism? What other resources are there?*

3. *Do you agree that there is a connection between vocation and liberal-arts study? Why or why not?*

4. *How can education address the needs of our students to be flexible and open to future vocational possibilities?*

5. *Does "spiritual formation" seem too pious or religious a term to describe what you do in your academic work?*

6. *Does scholarship and teaching seem like a spiritual endeavor to you? Why or why not?*

5   Student Faith Development

Throughout this book we have been looking at the relationship of faith and learning indirectly in the context of developing major themes in Lutheran higher education. It is now time to take a look at these issues directly—the complicated interaction between faith and learning particularly in the development of our students. Although this summary will not be exhaustive, it should be illustrative of the kinds of dimensions of learning that occur in our classrooms in regard to matters of faith. Being neither a developmental psychologist nor an educational theorist, I briefly will report some of what I have learned from others.

After looking at faith as a dynamic process, we will turn to a brief overview of faith development as a background to focusing specifically on the faith development stages of the traditional college-aged student. The hope is that this research will stimulate the reader to think about these matters and give some assistance in understanding where different students, and perhaps we, are when we enter the classroom.

I. FAITH AS A VERB

At least since the Middle Ages in the Christian tradition, it has been common to distinguish the content of faith (the object of devotion, that which is believed in) from the process of having faith (the process of expressing devotion, the means by which we believe). I find it helpful to think of this distinction not simply as a content and form distinction but as a grammatical one as well. Faith can be both a noun (the object of faith) and a verb (the process of engaging in faith commitment, "faithing").

For that reason faith also must be distinguished from "belief" and "religion." James Fowler, the founder of faith development research, observes that in more recent thought, belief has come to be equated with intellectual assent to propositional statements, particularly those that codify the doctrines or ideological claims of a particular tradition or group. Belief may be a part of a person's or group's faith, but it is only a part. Likewise, religion refers to the cumulative tradition composed of beliefs and practices that express and form the faith of people in the past or present.[1] Religion can include everything from art and architecture to symbols, rituals, narrative, myth, scriptures, doctrines, ethical teachings, music, and much more. If you will, religion can be viewed as the cultural embodiment of faith, but it is not identical to it. We turn, then, to a more generic and functional analysis of faith that focuses on process rather than on content, on faith as a verb.

Martin Luther was well aware of this distinction. Indeed in late medieval theology, faith had four aspects: *notitia* (knowledge), *assensus* (assent), *voluntas* (action of the will), and *fiducia* (trust). Luther was a practical and realistic thinker who, as he struggled with his own faith life, came to realize that trust (*fiducia*) ultimately encompassed all of the forms of faith. Without trust in God's justifying grace, none of the other expressions of faith were effective or meaningful. Luther's favorite definition of faith was Hebrews 11:1, "Now faith is the assurance of things hoped for, the conviction of things not seen." By employing this text he defined faith fundamentally as trust placed in the justifying grace of God. Faith is trust in that to which one gives ultimate devotion or loyalty.

Luther understood the subjective dynamics of faith and realized that our fundamental temptation was precisely to trust something other than God, which is idolatry. We will have faith. Being meaning-seeking creatures, we will create an object for our devotion if there is not one visible (for example, the story of the golden calf in Exodus 32). Commenting on this condition in the Large Catechism in regard to the First Commandment, Luther observes, "As I have often said, the trust and faith of the heart alone make both God and an idol. ... That to which your heart clings and entrusts itself is, I say, really your God."[2]

The issue, then, is what does one trust with one's life? Whatever one trusts and devotes one's time, energy, affection, and attention to *functions* as "god" for that person, regardless of what that object is. It can be anything from money and success to rock stars or the natural world. It also can be the God of the biblical tradition. When we come to see faith as a verb, as a process and function of the human, we realize that all people place their trust in something, through which their actions and life take on meaning. The focus at this point is on the process of devotion, not on the worthiness of the object of devotion.

The great twentieth-century theologian Paul Tillich developed Luther's understanding further for our time. He writes that faith is "ultimate concern,"[3] referring to that which concerns you ultimately, that one concern around which you center your life. Tillich observes, "Faith is a centered act of the whole human person. ... In faith reason reaches ecstatically beyond itself."[4] This process of faith involves all the capacities of the human. It is a fully committed trust and devotion, which fulfills the ultimate yearnings of reason by going beyond what reason alone can support and defend, without contradicting reason. It is the completion of the yearnings of both the human heart and mind. This also will necessarily involve doubt.

For Tillich there are three forms of doubt, only one of which relates to faith. There is *methodological* doubt, which arises from a method of scholarly study such as in the natural sciences. This doubt is programmatic in that it is built into the course of investigation and will be resolved if the study is successful. This is not the doubt of faith.

Second, there is *skeptical* doubt, that which questions everything at least for a brief time. Rene Descartes (1596–1650) is one of the greatest representatives of skeptical doubt in the West. In his *Meditations* he sought to question everything until he found his way back to an unquestioning foundation for belief. His famous conclusion "I think, therefore, I am" (*cogito ergo sum*) has been a paradigm for skeptical doubting ever since the seventeenth century. Descartes, however, did conclude that he could not question everything. Upon the basis of acknowledging his own thinking (to question that would be to question that he was questioning, which would be to cease questioning!), he then moved back to affirm much else in human life.[5] This also is not the doubt of faith.

For Tillich the doubt that is intrinsic to faith and is a structural feature of it is *existential* doubt, the uncertainty and anxiety based upon our very finitude. Existential doubt arises precisely when the finite attempts to commit itself to the infinite. As limited human creatures, we never can know with certainty that what we trust as our object of devotion is fully worthy of such trust. Since we never can infinitely know, feel, or experience in this life, there always will be an element of this doubt in every human expression of faith. It may not be on the surface and does not have to be present constantly, but it is there. For that reason Tillich sees faith as requiring courage. It is the courage to be in the face of our nonbeing, our mortality. It is not only the pain and loss of a friend or family member that makes the pathos of a funeral so intense. We know that at some other time, and thank God we do not know when, it will not be someone else in that casket, but it will be us—and what then? Where will we be? Whose will we be? Will we be?

Human beings live their lives in the dash, the dash inscribed on the grave marker between the date of birth and the date of death. Existential thinkers such as Tillich invite us to contemplate this dash and how and why we live it. Do we rush through it? Do we dash through the dash? It is interesting that such a terse and cryptic symbol comes to represent all the hopes and dreams, successes and failures, joys and sorrows of a human life. Perhaps its very brevity bespeaks the nature of our time, but we must not let it pass us by. Theologians such as Luther and Tillich invite us to pause and contemplate our lives and what we are committed to because this commitment affects all that we do, including our academic work and learning.

When we view faith as a verb, we begin to see that it is not optional but is of the quintessence of the human. While our feet are of the clay, our eyes and minds scan the stars. Humans exist juxtaposed between time and eternity, the finite and the infinite, in what I call the "mesocosmic"—the cosmic middle between the microcosmic and macrocosmic forces of existence. We find our place between quarks and quasars in such a fashion as to contemplate both. We are an example of the universe become self-conscious and able to reflect on time before its beginnings and after its demise.

This is what theologians at least partially mean by being created in the image of God. We all possess it, but all may not fully actualize it. We have it, our students have it, and it is part of the yearning that they bring when they enter our classrooms. It impinges on what they learn and on what we teach, and we all will be the better for it if we enter into that learning process self-conscious of our condition. When we recognize that the human process of meaning-seeking is at the core of what we have in mind by understanding faith (the verb) as a process, the possibility of relating faith and learning in the classroom opens up. To be truthful to academic freedom and the inspiring of human creativity, such a relating cannot be prescriptive or indoctrinating, but it can empower wonder, which is the most powerful engine for human learning and development.

II. FAITH DEVELOPMENT

Over the last several decades a number of cognitive and developmental theories have been formulated that have opened up the fascinating human process of learning. It is not my purpose to survey all of them, but I will highlight a few of the ideas that can be helpful in understanding the emerging field of faith development studies. While faith development research in the last twenty years has become its own bona fide field of study, it has grown out of developmental and cognitive psychology, particularly the works of Piaget,[6] Erikson,[7] Kohlberg,[8] and Selman.[9]

James W. Fowler is the founder of the discipline of faith development research, although many others, including William James, have investigated the psychological dynamics of faith. Fowler was the first one to intentionally develop a new discipline to investigate faith dynamics by drawing on the previously mentioned schools of thought. His former graduate student Sharon Daloz Parks has applied this approach directly to the young-adult life cycle and traditional college-aged students. We will look briefly at Fowler's understanding of the stages of faith development and then turn to Parks' treatment of college-aged young adults.

The focus of this overview is to help us grasp where our students (and we, for that matter) may be in their faith development to assist us in relating faith and learning. The intention is descriptive not prescriptive. It also must be said that this is not the only way of understanding faith development and that there are some criticisms of Fowler's approach, particularly as he attempts to merge a structuralist model (Piaget) with a psychosocial one (Erikson).[10] It is not our purpose to get into this internal debate but rather to indicate simply that one can talk about faith development in a clear and descriptive way that is approachable through clinical research and analysis. Undoubtedly further revisions of the approach will be made, but it is still a helpful starting point for understanding the diverse positions and needs concerning faith that enter through our classroom doors.

James Fowler has seven stages of faith development in which:

> *The stages aim to describe patterned operations of knowing and valuing that underlie our consciousness.* The varying stages of faith can be differentiated in relation to the degrees of complexity, of comprehensiveness, of internal differentiation, and of flexibility that their operations of knowing and valuing manifest. In continuity with constructive developmental tradition, faith stages are held to be *invariant, sequential,* and *hierarchical.* I do not claim for these stages *universality.*[11]

The seven stages are:

1. Primal faith (infancy)

2. Intuitive-projective faith (early childhood)

3. Mythic-literal faith (middle childhood and beyond)

4. Synthetic-conventional faith (adolescence and beyond)

5. Individuative-reflective faith (young adulthood and beyond)

6. Conjunctive faith (early mid-life and beyond)

7. Universalizing faith (mid-life and beyond)

Fowler makes the point that faith development includes a number of factors: biological maturation, emotional and cognitive development, psychosocial experience, and religio-cultural influences. He concludes, "Because development in faith involves aspects of all these sectors of human growth and change, movement from one stage to another is not automatic or assured. Persons may reach chronological and biological adulthood while remaining defined by structural stages of faith that would most commonly be associated with early or middle childhood or adolescence."[12] He also goes on to indicate that a transition from one stage to another does not necessarily mean a change in the content or direction of one's faith but rather in the way one holds, understands, and takes responsibility for one's faith.[13]

Primal faith is prelinguistic and grounded in the care given to the infant. It offsets the anxiety that results from separations that occur during infant development. If infants' needs are met, they will develop a trust of adults and the world. Dependability in having their needs met confirms them as being "at home" in their life spaces, but if significant deficits occur they can give rise to a foundational mistrust of self, others, and the larger environment.[14] Recent neurophysiological research also has found that there are profound physiological developments that emerge in these early years as the brain is "wired" for future developments in areas such as mathematics, language, music, and so forth. Lack of stimulation in these early years can lead to truncated development in later life.[15]

Intuitive-projective faith begins with the use of language, symbols, stories, dreams, and the imagination. Not yet controlled by logical thinking, this stage combines perception and feeling to create long-lasting images that represent both the protective and threatening powers surrounding one's life. At this stage a child cannot distinguish fantasy from fact, but there is in this stage the possibility of aligning powerful religious symbols and images with deep feelings of terror and guilt or of love and companionship. It is in this stage that children develop their first representations of God. Fowler observes that should a splitting or a dissociation occur with the parents at this time through abuse, neglect, or divorce, it can lead to the construction of a "bad" self deserving of the punishment from the "just" God. He comments, "In faith terms this correlates with constructions of God along the lines of a taskmaster deity who requires performance and perfection, or shame and guilt about failures, for one to qualify for grace and approval."[16] Clearly the early upbringing of children significantly impacts their religious outlooks for good or ill.

With *mythic-literal* faith, we enter the first stage of faith that, although it begins in middle childhood, can persist into adulthood. Here Piaget's "concrete operational" stage of cognitive development is found, and it makes for the conscious interpretation and shaping of experiences and meanings. Fowler observes, "In this Mythic-Literal stage, the child, adolescent, or adult does not yet construct the interiority—the feelings, attitudes, and internal guiding processes—of the self or others. Similarly, one does not construct God in particularly personal terms, or attribute to God highly differentiated internal emotions and interpersonal sensitivities. In making sense of the larger order of things, therefore, this stage typically structures the ultimate environment—the cosmic pattern of God's rule or control of the universe—along the lines of simple fairness and moral reciprocity."[17]

People in this stage engage effectively in narrative, although they do not place themselves in the flow of the narrative itself. They do not carry out extensive synthetic reflection about themselves or their own stories. The use of symbols remains largely concrete and literal. The transition to the next stage begins when these people—whether children, adolescents, or adults—experience bad things happening to good people and see that evil people do not necessarily suffer for their transgressions. It becomes impossible to maintain the concept of a God built along the lines of simple moral retribution. This may lead to a temporary or permanent giving up of belief in God.

In the *synthetic-conventional* stage of faith, the young person also enters into the full-blown physiological impact of adolescence. With the emergence of early formal operational thinking (Piaget), a young person's thought becomes capable of appreciating abstract concepts, and she or he begins to think about thinking and to name and synthesize meanings. Also at this point there is the emergence of mutual interpersonal perspective taking (Selman) so that identity and personal interiority become absorbing concerns. Fowler observes, "During this stage youths develop attachments to beliefs, values and elements of personal style that link them in conforming relations with the most significant others among their peers, family and other adults." But "at this stage, one's ideology or worldview is lived and asserted; it is not yet a matter of critical and reflective articulation."[18]

It is also at this time that certain deficits from earlier childhood can come to inhibit cognitive abilities in the task of identity construction. At this point the potential of God as a constructive self-object may have to be jettisoned because God may only be seen in regard to the emotionally shaming and narcissistic qualities of earlier childhood. Fowler concludes, "One decisive limit of the Synthetic-Conventional stage is its lack of *third-person perspective taking*. … The self does not yet have a transcendental perspective from which it can see and evaluate self-other *relations*. In the Synthetic-Conventional stage the young person or adult can remain trapped in the 'Tyranny of the They.'"[19] This explains why, while this developmental stage does involve synthesis, it still is heavily tied to the thoughts and feelings of others and feels the pressure of the conventional. It is with the next stage that truly individual reflection develops.

Fowler found that for *individuative-reflective* faith to emerge, two very important movements must occur. First the previous stage's tacit system of beliefs, values, and commitments must be examined critically and second, the personal identity developed must now become defined independently of the earlier conditioning relationships.[20] People in this stage become reflective about both their worldviews and their personal relationships as they begin to assert their own personal identities and take over personal authority for themselves, a role previously conducted by others. At the heart of this double movement is the emergence of *third-person perspective taking*, which was lacking in the previous stage. This perspective permits a transcendental view of self-other relations and a standpoint from which to adjudicate conflicting expectations as one's own inner authority develops. One then is capable of codifying frames of meaning that are conscious of their own boundaries and inner connections so that people at this stage can "demythologize" symbols, rituals, and myths, translating their meanings into conceptual formulations. Clearly at this stage one has entered the phase of critical awareness and thinking.

The danger at this stage is in developing the cognitive but not the affective dimensions of life. A person may be at this stage cognitively but at an earlier stage emotionally. This can lead to limited empathy and emotional insensitivity to others while at the same time becoming very confident of one's worldview and authority. Fowler observes, "Religiously, these persons are often drawn to the rigidities and seemingly unambiguous teachings of Fundamentalism and of authoritarian leaders."[21] This need not happen, of course, if there can be congruence between the cognitive and the affective dimensions, but an imbalance and lack of attention to one's own unconscious processes eventually may lead to burnout due to the energy expended to maintain the dissonance between cognitive self-identity and a conflicting emotional one. Such congruent unity is the hallmark of the next stage.

Conjunctive faith in many respects requires the dismantling of some of the clearly defined boundaries produced in the earlier stage. It is a stage in which the "coincidence of opposites" (from Nicolas of Cusa, 1401–64) are found to be present in our apprehension of truth. One becomes aware that truth may be approached from a number of different perspectives and that one's own identity is heavily dependent upon unconscious as well as conscious forces. Fowler comments,

> We *have* a conscious mind, but we also *are* a great deal of patterned action and reaction that is largely unconscious. ... Faith must learn to maintain the tensions between these multiple perspectives, refusing to collapse them in one direction or another. In this sense, faith must begin to come to terms with indissoluble paradoxes: the strength found in apparent weakness; the leadership that is possible from the margins of societies and groups not from the center; the immanence *and* the transcendence of God. Conjunctive faith exhibits a kind of epistemological humility. ... This stage marks a movement beyond the demythologizing strategy of the Individuative-Reflective stage. Acknowledging the multidimensionality and density of symbols and myth, persons in the Conjunctive stage learn to enter into symbolic realities, allowing them to exert their illuminating and mediating power.[22]

People in this stage display what philosopher Paul Ricoeur calls the "second" or "willed" naïveté. Having passed through critical analysis of their faith, they are ready to enter the rich meanings of true symbols, myths, and ritual in a clear move beyond the demythologizing strategy of the earlier stage. As a correlate, this stage also exhibits a principled openness to the truths of other religious and faith traditions.[23] Clearly this is a mature and rich stage of faith development—one which many of us would be fortunate to achieve, but Fowler does open up the possibility of one last stage.

Universalizing faith is possible but rare. "This stage involves persons moving beyond the paradoxical awareness and embrace of polar opposites that are hallmarks of the Conjunctive stage. The structuring of this stage derives from the radical completion of a process of de-centration from self that proceeds throughout the sequence of stages."[24] Gradually the circle of those who count in faith, in the making of meaning and the doing of justice, is expanded to the point where an all-pervading inclusiveness is reached. There is a degree of saintliness associated with such people because the self in this stage has moved beyond the usual forms of defensiveness and exhibits an openness grounded in the being, love, and regard of God. These people can be distinguished from the destructive charismatic leaders such as at Jonestown or Waco because they do not build up a regressive dependence upon themselves or require a relinquishing of personal responsibility from their followers. Fowler concludes, "Persons of this stage are as concerned with the transformation of those they oppose as with the bringing about of justice and reform." Mother Teresa, the Dalai Lama, Dom Heldar Camara, and Jimmy Carter would be current examples of such a universalizing faith.[25]

The purpose of this overview has been to give us a sense of the types of stages and movements that may be found in faith development analysis. Fowler strives to indicate that he wants these stages to be seen as descriptive not prescriptive, although his use of the structural model of Piaget, among others, makes it hard not to see one stage as more fulfilling and complete than the previous. Indeed this is the very nature of developmental theories in psychology as well. Clearly there is some physiological chronology involved because in his research he has not seen the stages he describes at an age prior to those that he indicates. But it also must be said that development in faith is not simply linear. It is more of a spiral,[26] a cycle that may return to questions and issues time and again as one reappropriates, revises, and perhaps rejects the faith content of one's tradition. For our purposes here, Fowler's overall theory is to be seen as background to addressing the question of the faith stages of our students and the faith issues that they may bring into our classrooms, regardless of the subject being studied. The traditional college-aged student is embarking on the critical years of the transition to young adulthood.

III. THE CRITICAL YEARS

The title for this section comes from the work of Sharon Daloz Parks, who has applied Fowler's theory directly to traditional college-aged young adults.[27] Her conclusion is that the majority of students we see are in the transition from stages four to five—synthetic-conventional to individuative-reflective. There still may be some at the mythic-literal stage as well. If you have nontraditional-aged students in your classes, as many of us do, there even could be elements of conjunctive faith present, too, although age is no guarantee of development. Our classrooms, in other words, are a bubbling diversity of faith development perspectives so that any mentioning of faith issues usually will elicit quite diverse and intense responses, making many faculty hesitant to bring up the subject at all!

I hope that the discussion of these stages of faith and the developmentally diverse perspectives they represent will encourage you to consider bringing faith questions into the classroom. The potential gains in growth and dialogue far outweigh the possible confusion that might result. If our students do not receive thoughtful and articulate models of faith in colleges of the church (where reasonable and civil discourse about religious matters should be present), where will they get it? Our society does not readily foster it, and the church does not have the educational resources to fully embody the discussions across disciplinary lines. This is one of the most unique and critical contributions that colleges of the church can make to the spiritual growth of its students.

Parks sees that some further discernment within Fowler's model is necessary if we truly are to address the complex and subtle faith development taking place in the students in front of our podiums. Drawing upon the thought of Perry and Erikson as well as Fowler, she argues for an additional stage within the movement from adolescence to adult faith. She sees this as more than merely "transitional"—it actually constitutes its own developmental level. She names this stage "*identity*" and sees it as the culmination point of adolescence (Erikson) and the beginning of adult development: "The achievement of 'identity' marks the threshold of adulthood."[28]

This achievement occurs within the development from the synthetic-conventional to the individuative-reflective stages of faith and in the middle of our classrooms. It occurs as the defining movement to young adulthood and has cognitive, dependency, communal, and religious dimensions. Parks' insight was developed through her work as a religion professor and a campus chaplain for college students, as well as through her studies with William Perry and cognitive development theory.[29] She condenses and modifies Perry's nine stages of intellectual and moral development into four for simplicity and clarity, and to develop parallels between the forms of cognition and forms of dependence and community.[30]

Her four-fold schema[31] looks like this:

Form of cognition:	Authority-bound dualistic	→	Unqualified relativism	→	Commitment in relativism	→	Convictional commitment
Form of dependence:	Dependent/counter dependent			→	Inner-dependent	→	Inter-dependent
Form of community:	Conventional	→	Diffuse	→	Self-selected	→	Open to other
Form of faith:	Egypt	→	Wilderness	→	Spirit within	→	Promised Land

Instead of summarizing this schema, I will focus primarily on the forms of cognition because of the intellectual character of college education. Brief mention will be made of the dependency structures as well since they are a clue to feelings. Cognition gives us access to what a person *thinks* and dependence to what a person *feels.* Human beings are necessarily interdependent beings, but the form of experience and awareness of dependence changes as we develop.[32] It must be kept in mind, however, that with the cognitive and dependency changes there also are parallel developments in community and faith as indicated in the above schema.

As was mentioned toward the end of the last chapter, when most of our students begin college they are in Perry's dualistic phase. They assume that there is only one right answer and it is the professor's task to give it to them. At this stage of cognitive development, the encouragement to self-reflection for many seems beside the point. They simply assume that there is one answer that we are wanting them to ferret out. This also explains the traditional first-year student questions: "Will this be on the test?" "Do you really want us to know this?" It is important to observe that this cognitive state correlated for Parks with the synthetic-conventional state of faith. God is in the heavens and all is right with the world—at least until they meet their first college roommate. Here too there is a state of dependence because the authority is still external to the self and the student tacitly is accepting the worldview of that authority—professor, parent, pastor, and so forth. This all changes as the conventional structure breaks down, usually right in our classrooms.

It should not be surprising, then, that when this conventional super-structure (read "worldview") starts to weaken, there is an easy free-fall into full-blown unqualified relativism. "You have a truth. I have a truth. It doesn't matter what one believes as long as they are sincere." This position, of course, is an attempt to still hold sincerity out as an absolute, but this comes crashing down when it is pointed out that Hitler also was sincere in his vision of the truth.

Others, of course, will fight tenaciously for their position and assume you are either wrong, malevolent, or blind if you do not affirm conventional truth. (This is usually where religion and philosophy faculty get accused of heresy.) The young adult is attempting to chart her or his own way between the Scylla of increasingly inadequate dualism (a clearly defined right and wrong) on the one hand and the Charybdis of unqualified relativism (any truth is as good as another) on the other (with its close companion of meaninglessness). Little wonder that their questions and pronouncements may become intense! As William Perry observes, "It is not for nothing that the undergraduate turns metaphysician."[33] This stage usually is accompanied by the move to counter-dependence as they begin to assert their own intellectual and emotional autonomy. It also can feel like a wilderness, for the usual guideposts are gone. Relativism, for the moment, seems to win the day.

One cannot live forever in unqualified relativism, however. As Parks observes, "One discovers that there is a difference between just an opinion and an opinion that is grounded in careful, thoughtful observation and reflection. One may move into a more qualified relativism, increasingly aware that discriminations can be made between arguments based on such principles as internal coherence, the systematic relation of an argument to its own assumptions, external data, and so forth."[34]

One must and does get on with one's life, and here is where the transition to commitment in relativism begins. Students come to realize, "There are many options and so now, for myself, I must choose." It is here that the breaking down of the synthetic-conventional faith moves toward the individuative-reflective. Parks, agreeing with Fowler, states that what is happening is that a person is moving from a "tacit" to an "explicit" system of understanding.[35] One is beginning to take self-conscious responsibility for one's knowing, shifting from a worldview that is tacit and unreflectively appropriated to one that is intended to make explicit the meaning in one's life for oneself. Parks contends that it is this movement that is *most characteristic of the young adult in the university years.*[36] If we are creative, honest, and forthcoming—really professing what we know as true to the best of our ability—with our students, they will grow and begin to put their own lives together anew.

Mentoring—this is where self-selected significant mentors and peers become essential. Parks observes that the dependency state moves here not to independence but to what she refers to as inner-dependence. She observes, "In other words, other sources of authority may still hold credible power, but now one can recognize and value also the authority of the self."[37] Here is where co-inquiry really takes off with students, and one senses a fellow sojourner on the educational journey. Mentoring becomes essential to provide the support the fledgling individual reflection and commitment need to develop. Mentors anchor the vision of the potential self and by so doing provide a ground for commitment within relativism for the student.[38]

This is as true in matters of faith as it is in scholarly disciplines and is why the avoidance of faith questions can be so deleterious to our students' spiritual, and perhaps cognitive and emotional, development. The structure of faith development needs content if there is to be true moral development as well. Carol Gilligan, in her work in modifying the moral development theory of Lawrence Kohlberg, comes to the same conclusion.[39] Parks concludes, "Once we recognize that the structure of young adult faith mandates a search for an 'authentic' basis of moral action and that this search can be fulfilled by 'contents' as diverse as hedonism, cynical moral nihilism, or an ethics of service to others, then we see that an understanding of development defined in merely structural terms can only be a part of what we seek."[40] One can inform without indoctrinating. One can confess without proselytizing. One can assist in providing content for the faith development process as well as assist in its structural growth.

We will not be with our students long enough to see them reach convictional commitment and inter-dependence. These usually emerge after mid-life, when people come to realize that they have lived more than half of their lives.[41] Our window of opportunity occurs in this identity stage that Parks characterizes as "probing commitment."[42] At this stage the young adult is moving to individual inner-dependence in reflection and emotion as well as in faith. It is here that the interaction of faith and learning is critical. Colleges of the church are well-suited to address such a transition, and it is an essential part of our mission to do so. There are no other educational contexts in society with the same resources, commitment, and faith traditions as church-related colleges. *If we do not do it; it will not get done.* Far from an interference in our scholarly commitments, it is one of our central callings as we mentor and model for our students the ways in which we make meaning in our own lives.

QUESTIONS FOR REFLECTION

1. *How would you define faith? Is the distinction between the content and function of faith a helpful one for you? What does it mean to refer to faith as a verb or a process, in your opinion?*

2. *What is your response to the analysis of the stages of faith development? Do you find this theory helpful in understanding your students? Yourself?*

3. *At which stage(s) would you find most of your students, do you think? Find yourself?*

4. *Do you find Parks' analysis of student cognitive development useful?*

5. *Do you think that we have a responsibility to assist our students in moral and faith development? Why or why not?*

6. *How would you describe the process of mentoring? When, where, how, and by whom should it be done?*

6   Pedagogical Issues

The discussion of student cognitive and faith development in the previous chapter naturally leads to a consideration of pedagogical issues. If student development is considered the end, what are the means? A myriad of issues could be addressed, but for the sake of space I have selected four that to me are most salient for a church-related college: academic freedom, Christian presence, postmodern pedagogy, and community ethos. Elements of pedagogical method are implicit within these issues, but disciplinary methodologies vary so widely that I thought it best to leave methodology up to the expertise of the individual instructor. I am sure there are other issues that you would like to address as you discuss the questions at the end of the chapter.

I. ACADEMIC FREEDOM IN A POSTMODERN CONTEXT

Academic freedom is essential to the pursuit of truth and the life of the mind. Without such freedom intellectual life can fall victim to imposed ideology and the constraints of pragmatic interests alone. It also is essential for the cultivation of the liberal arts. Within the Lutheran tradition academic freedom is understood as an academic application of the doctrine of the two kingdoms—the distinction between the world of today and the world to come in regard to God's governance. (Please see "Luther and Learning," Chapter 2, section 1.) Today reason dominates as the means to study the order God has placed in creation, thus granting each discipline its own integrity and freedom.[1] The integrity of creation requires nothing less than the integrity and freedom of disciplines devoted to its study. Only in this way can a healthy and constructive dialectical relationship between the two kingdoms of nature and grace be maintained, allowing for the pursuit of truth.

What is sought here is *not* a "Christian biology" or "Christian physics" but rather a dynamic interrelationship between biology, physics, or any discipline and the Christian faith. One discipline does not dictate to another, but a relationship of mutual respect and integrity is maintained. *Academic freedom must be conserved in order to maintain the critical task of understanding life in this world.* On the other hand, as contemporary epistemological critiques have shown, there is no such thing as a perspectiveless or neutral framework of meaning and interpretation, even in the public university. Therefore it is not a violation of academic freedom or integrity for a college of the church to attempt to bring scholarly reflection into relationship with Christian perspectives. This leads us to a constructive task regarding academic freedom.

Over the last twenty-five to thirty years an awareness of the limits of Enlightenment reflection and the Cartesian/Newtonian paradigm for thought has been developing. The belief that one could construct or derive a purely objective, neutral, bias-free, and rational perspective on any subject of discourse is now coming to be seen as a dream forged in the myth of an ahistorical reality. All thought is contextual and therefore all facts are value laden. Facts are contextual truths that arise precisely through a framework of interpretation that allows raw data to be connected for the construction of meaning. This does not mean that there is no truth; it means that the true, like the real, is always encountered from and defined by a particular perspective. To suspend belief in order to understand is now seen as an impossible task—"foundationalism" as Richard Rorty refers to it[2]—or "objectivism" as Parker Palmer calls it. Palmer observes, "Objectivism begins by assuming a sharp distinction between the knower and the objects to be known. These objects exist 'out there,' apart from and independent of the knower."[3]

It is precisely this separation between the knower and the known that has fallen under radical critique in our day. Coming initially out of the philosophy of science, it is argued that no rigid distinction can be made between the two and that every scientific finding is a mixture of both subjective and objective elements (see Barbour and Pannenberg). The task now is not to deny perspective and context in thought but to become more inclusively aware of what actually informs one's thought. Palmer's indictment of objectivism stems from his insight that epistemologies have moral trajectories—that ways of knowing are not morally neutral but morally directive. He sees learning as a communal exercise in which knowing is understood as a spiritual form of relationship ultimately bound together by love.[4]

In regard to the area of academic freedom, what this means is that it is not an intellectual faux pas to attempt to connect one's religious faith to other realms of learning. There is always some faith position present, even if it is faith in reason alone. Academic freedom does *not* mean absolute neutrality in learning and reflection but rather the free and open debate and dialogue between various perspectives of learning, the various personal and social contexts in which knowing takes place.

Ernie Trashes the myth of objectivity

Academic freedom assures an open playing field. It does not mean that there are no teams on the field. Christian scholars, then, need not apologize for their Christianity any more than should a Buddhist, Jewish, Islamic, or secular scholar. Secularism is only one alternative belief structure for the construction and interpretation of reality. It is not the only one. As George Marsden, among others, has pointed out, there is no value-free inquiry anywhere, including at the university, and so, just as other voices need to be brought to bear in scholarly discourse, so too should the Christian voice be a member of the conversation.[5] This is not to make an intellectual sacrifice but to acknowledge one's basis of existence as essential to one's thought.

In all the discussions of the limits of the Enlightenment we also must be careful not to give up its great contributions to Western culture, including the role of reason in formulating more generally held attributes of analysis and understanding. We must not allow a critique of rationalism to allow us to fall back into the abyss of irrationalism. While all thought is contextual, this does not intrinsically preclude the possibility of some commonly shared principles of understanding and conduct across contextual lines, otherwise social order and democracy as we know it become impossible. In theory the postmodern critique affirms academic freedom and permits the legitimate introduction of other perspectives, including the religious. This development is a direct result of the emergence of pluralism, to which I will now turn in relation to Christian presence and the mission of the church.

II. CHRISTIAN PRESENCE IN A PLURALISTIC SOCIETY

As colleges of the church, our institutions should assure that there will be a Christian presence, a Christian voice, in the intellectual conversation on campus. Yes, this is to privilege one perspective, not by giving it the final word but by assuring that it will be present in the conversation. This faith/learning dialogue would occur especially in the classroom, where Christian thought is brought into relationship with every discipline on campus in whatever manner is appropriate to the discipline. There it should be critiqued and evaluated for its value and truthfulness as with any perspective on life and thought. Christianity has no fear of the truth, and if certain insights need modification in light of new understanding, that modification should take place.[6]

One of the most important services that colleges can render to the church is to sustain its faith tradition in dynamic interrelationship with contemporary life and thought. As Robert Jenson observes, "A college of the church will try to be for its students and faculty a true public realm, a community of discourse and virtue, even as around it such realms collapse."[7] To see all life and thought within the context of God's law and governance can provide a basis for holistic integration at a time in society when fragmentation is the norm. This is not to dictate belief to the wider society but to assist individuals, our students, and ourselves, in seeing that "in him all things hold together" (Colossians 1:17). The model supported here is that of a "Free Christian College," in the earlier Danforth Commission typology in which there is an open and free exchange of perspectives. This is not the "Defender of the Faith" model in which free discussion is prevented by forced doctrinal subscription.[8] (See the Lutheran model for Christian higher education discussed in Chapter 3.) This raises the issue of religious and cultural pluralism on our campuses.

There has been a great deal written on pluralism, and I will not bore you with a rehash of that. Cultural and religious pluralism is a reality of our social context. Drawing upon a distinction made by systematic theologian Ted Peters and the recent discussion of "culture wars," I would like to speak of two forms of pluralism—"descriptive pluralism" and "dogmatic or radical pluralism."[9] Peters defines descriptive pluralism as "the side-by-side existence of various and contradictory perspectives, worldviews, or approaches to human understanding and living. … Descriptive pluralism describes the situation in which we find ourselves."[10] Dogmatic pluralism, on the other hand, is prescriptive pluralism because it consists "of a positive affirmation of pluralism as a way of viewing reality that dictates conceptual and ethical commitments. It holds that variety and diversity are positive goods and that the denial of variety and diversity is bad."[11]

Pluralism, of course, is not new. The motto *e pluribus unum* reflects the two-hundred-year-old commitment of the United States to be the embodiment of a peaceable pluralism. What is new is the recognition of the *required participation* of the voices of the other into our cultural and intellectual conversation. This has been an enriching and informing experience and is much preferred to the hegemonistic political and intellectual oppression that occurred in the past. This is the positive value of descriptive pluralism. It was made possible to a large extent by the Enlightenment emphases upon reason and toleration as grounding principles for social and intellectual life. Today, however, in the name of dogmatic pluralism, toleration itself is becoming threatened.

Peters (and also James Davison Hunter in his book *Culture Wars*) makes the point that pluralism in its other, dogmatic form is taking additional turns today that may preclude critical appraisal and moral formation. Peters writes that when pushed to its extreme, "radical pluralism so embraces cultural relativism that no universal value regarding 'the good' or vision of what fulfills human aspiration can be mounted. Radical pluralism so affirms the integrity of a given perspective that any attempt to change is considered a cultural violation."[12] The question raised here is whether this radical form of pluralism can be coherent as a value system without commitment to some form of universal humanity?

The questions this raises for institutions such as colleges is nothing less than the ongoing possibility of rational discourse. Dogmatically affirmed, radical plurality separates and forces each speaker into a form of self-contained cultural contextualism that does not permit critique or affirmation from without. In such a context intellectual life comes to a halt because unbridgeable separation between human groups is maintained to the denial of any common humanity. The issue is not whether there will be pluralism, but rather, pluralism of which form? I believe the collapse of radical pluralism into the abyss of ethical solipsism indicates its limited utility for human social understanding and therefore should be rejected.

Pluralism also impacts the understanding of the church's mission. Theologically the mission of the church is to proclaim the gospel and bear witness to her Lord through both word and deed. Precisely how that is to be done today in a pluralistic setting is one of the most critical challenges to the church and one that directly impacts how colleges can be related to the church. The decline in membership of mainline Protestant denominations during the last twenty to thirty years is a well-known fact (see Woodward and Johnson). What is less clear—and the subject of much scrutiny and debate—are the causes for such decline.

In his book *The Once and Future Church*, Loren Meade, former president of the Alban Institute in Washington, D.C., argues that we are in the midst of a major paradigm shift in the mission of the church. We have moved from an "Apostolic Paradigm," in which the mission field was the front door of the church, to the "Christendom Paradigm," in which the mission field is the frontier of the empire. Meade believes we have been in the breakdown of the Christendom Paradigm for some time now, perhaps since the beginning of the Reformation.[13]

Confusion about the proper location of the mission field of the church is one indicator of this paradigm shift at work. Another is the shift in support given to national and international structures, most of which were founded to support a different paradigm of mission. Meade believes that it will take several more generations to formulate the new paradigm, but he sees signs of it all around, including congregations that take it upon themselves to address local needs such as day care, homelessness, racism, and domestic violence in their communities. The mission field is not only the front street for many congregations but also the front pew, where "inreach" (in contrast to outreach to the wider society) to support suffering members is a critical ministry. Colleges of the church can play an important role in helping the church formulate a new paradigm of mission precisely by giving to the church thoughtful reflection on the character and nature of forces at work in the world.

Such forces certainly have impacted the character of our students. Any of us who have been around the academy for a while are aware that there have been changes in the background knowledge and learning styles of our students. Students continue to be intelligent and, for the most part, open to learning, even if it is driven by occupational concerns. My sense, however, is that students do not know as much when they come to college now as they used to, particularly in the area of the humanities, including knowledge of Western cultural history and the biblical narrative. Research also indicates that most of them are concrete active learners; only about ten percent are abstractive reflective learners, which is what most college faculty are.[14] As a professor of religion seeking informed understanding about theology, I find myself doing more remediation in the biblical and historical traditions than I used to. When I have some students who think Moses was a disciple and Martin Luther was a civil-rights leader, I have to change my educational agenda.

These are glaring examples, of course, and not the norm, but I still have the clear impression that our students today know more and more about less and less. Perhaps this is the effect of disciplinary specialization or students raised on sound bytes, photo opportunities, and *Sesame Street* attention spans. There is a lack of extended, in-depth reflection in the mass media and the wider public arena of discussion. But I sense the problem is deeper. I do not blame the students, nor am I looking for someone else to blame, whether it be public schools, parish education, or parents. There is enough responsibility to go around for all. What to me seems at stake in this is nothing less than an informed understanding of religion and the continuation of cultural literacy. E. D. Hirsch's book *Cultural Literacy* is a case in point to the national discussion of this concern.

It is, of course, related to the issues of pluralism discussed earlier, and those of us in the education field especially need to be concerned.

The liberal arts historically have been the repositories of meaning, identity, and preparation for civic responsibility in the West. Those tasks are all the greater today as we seek to chart for both ourselves and our students a course through the bewildering matrix of cultural and educational debates. Do the liberal arts have a canon any longer? Or is the word "canon" a euphemism for cultural imperialism? If there is no canon of meaning, can there then be any acceptable standard of conduct or social interchange? Are public discourse and debate simply to be replaced by badgering, posturing, and misinformation? Is political debate reduced to being a Larry King circus sideshow? These kinds of questions lead Robert Jenson to suggest that the mission of the church college is "in the name of God to save our culture from itself."[15]

I am sensing that many in our society are concerned about these issues and from many different social contexts, including the African American community. This certainly is part of what is behind theologian Cornel West's *Race Matters* and its unexpectedly wide readership. Yale law professor Stephen Carter's *The Culture of Disbelief* also strikes some similar themes. For him religion seems to be marginalized as a private affair by the intellectual establishment, thereby undercutting a traditional basis for public morality.[16] In such a culture of disbelief, Carter argues that God is treated as a "hobby" (Chapter 2) and anyone who attempts to take religion seriously in public life is treated as a fanatic.[17] Colleges of the church have a real stake in this discussion. On our campuses, perhaps, if nowhere else in our society, religious beliefs should be raised, discussed, and critiqued in an informed manner that does not dismiss them as a hobby or label them as fanatical. Our society desperately needs informed and reasonable discussion of religious beliefs, and our students bring that same need with them when they come to our campuses.

III. TOWARD A POSTMODERN PEDAGOGY

Throughout this book it has been observed that we are living in a time of critique of modernist Enlightenment assumptions regarding foundationalism (the formulation of objective, universal, and rationally self-evident truths) and the ability of reason to reflect in an objective, neutral, and universal way about reality. All thought is contextual and all facts are value laden. Many postmodern and feminist critiques have revealed the implicit imperialism, hegemony, discrimination, and power relations that are present in metanarratives written or endorsed by the dominant power groups. They have been tools to legitimate exploitation and subservience of large sectors of society. Whenever anyone says, "This is just the way things are," one must always stop and ask who are the beneficiaries of that status quo position.

Although all knowledge is perspectival, not all perspective is knowledge. Perspective is relative essentially; it would not be perspective without it. But knowledge is relative only conditionally, to the perspective from which it originates, and in all other cases is objective such that its claims can be testable and falsifiable.[18] So acknowledging perspective does not mean a collapse into indiscriminate relativism or nihilism. It does mean multicultural dialogue, the denial of positivism, and an awareness of the power-relating, socializing role that education plays in society.

Henry A. Giroux, an educational theorist at Pennsylvania State University, has been thinking about postmodern social criticism in relation to educational theory for more than twenty years and offers what he calls a "Critical Pedagogy" as a constructive response.[19] He seeks to overcome the binary, adversarial relationship between modernity and postmodernity as well as include the insights of feminist criticism. He is an articulate advocate for a radical and ethical democracy in which education plays a key role in the preparation of its citizens. To encourage reflection on pedagogical assumptions, I would like to list Giroux's nine principles for a critical pedagogy and comment on a few of them. They have many stimulating implications for church-related higher education as well as wider social criticism. Giroux's assumption is that "we live in a time in which the responsibilities of citizens transcend national borders."[20] The pedagogy we employ must reflect this changed context. His nine principles[21] are:

1. Education must be understood as producing not only knowledge but also political subjects.

2. Ethics must be seen as a central concern of critical pedagogy.

3. Critical pedagogy needs to focus on the issue of difference in an ethically challenging and politically transformative way.

4. Critical pedagogy needs a language that allows for competing solidarities and political vocabularies that do not reduce the issues of power, justice, struggle, and inequality to a single script or a master narrative that suppresses the contingent, the historical, and the everyday as serious objects of study.

5. Critical pedagogy needs to create new forms of knowledge through its emphasis on breaking down disciplinary boundaries and creating new spaces where knowledge can be produced.

6. The Enlightenment notion of reason needs to be reformulated within a critical pedagogy.

7. Critical pedagogy needs to regain a sense of alternatives by combining the languages of critique and possibility.

8. Critical pedagogy needs to develop a theory of teachers as transformative intellectuals who occupy specifiable political and social locations.

9. Central to the notion of critical pedagogy is a politics of voice that combines a postmodern notion of difference with a feminist emphasis on the primacy of the political.

The first principle simply acknowledges the historical and political purpose of education, which is to support political democracy by preparing a "public sphere of citizens" who are able to exercise power over their own lives. This then requires a central concern for ethics that offer students diverse ethical referents for structuring their relationship to the wider society. Giroux insists, "Educators must also come to view ethics and politics as a relationship between the self and the other. Ethics, in this case, is not a matter of individual relativism but a social discourse grounded in struggles that refuse to accept needless human suffering and exploitation."[22] He wants to see this as an ethics that is rooted neither in essentialism nor relativism but in historical struggles and is attentive to the construction of social relations free of injustice.

By employing multiple narratives, this pedagogy seeks to break down disciplinary boundaries so that students can see diverse cultural involvement. Giroux remarks, "At stake here is a pedagogy that provides the knowledge, skills, and habits for students and others to read history in ways that enable them to reclaim their identities in the interest of constructing forms of life that are more democratic and more just. This struggle deepens the pedagogical meaning of the political and the political meaning of the pedagogical. In the first instance, it raises important questions about how students and others are constructed as agents within particular histories, cultures and social relations."[23] This would make explicit the role schools play in shaping and legitimizing particular identities, values, and histories and permit part of the "critical" function of the pedagogy.

This is supplemented by a reformulated Enlightenment understanding of reason that does not purport to reveal the truth by denying its own historical construction and ideological principles. Giroux observes, "This suggests that we reject claims to objectivity in favor of partial epistemologies that recognize the historical and socially constructed nature of their own knowledge claims and methodologies. In this way, curriculum can be viewed as a cultural script that introduces students to particular forms of reason that structure specific stories and ways of life. Reason in this sense implicates and is implicated in the intersection of power, knowledge and politics."[24] Reason is not innocent or beyond criticism, but neither should it be abandoned.

This then would allow pedagogy to regain a sense of alternatives by combining its languages of critique and possibility. Giroux sees feminism and its critique of patriarchy as a model for such a critical approach that also offers possibility. It does not simply critique but also attempts to envision and even construct. He is particularly critical of the cynicism that is so prevalent in the language of the Left at this time, which refuses utopian images and the "language of possibility." Giroux observes, "In contrast to the language of dystopia, a discourse of possibility rejects apocalyptic emptiness and nostalgic imperialism and sees history as open and society worth struggling for in the image of an alternative future. This is the language of the 'not yet,' one in which imagination is redeemed and nourished in the effort to construct new relationships fashioned out of strategies of collective resistance based upon a critical recognition of both what society is and what it might become."[25] Giroux here echoes the thought of many liberation thinkers, including liberation theologians who see the power of the future to lie precisely in its ability to envision alternative possibilities that can stand in critique of what is.

Again, it is in light of what might be that one can become empowered to change what is. If one has no vision of the future, no vision of possibility, then one is left with the status quo, which one must either reconcile with or attempt to destroy. Criticism without alternative possibility is simply parasitic, lacking any life of its own. Criticism with alternative possibility, however, can be transformative. It is to the transformative intellectual task that Giroux calls all educators.

Finally, Giroux seeks a pedagogy of voice that takes up the personal and the political in a way that does not collapse the political into the personal, "but strengthens the relationship between the two so as to engage in rather than withdraw from addressing those institutional forms and structures that contribute to forms of racism, sexism, and class exploitation."[26] Liberation thinkers for years, especially in Latin America, have talked about a pedagogy that gives "voice to the voiceless,"[27] and Giroux's pedagogy attempts to do this in a constructive way. This view of voice first sees the self as the primary site of politicization and second offers pedagogical and political strategies that affirm the primacy of the social, intersubjective, and collective. This involves more than simply naming one's experience or affirming the stories of students and glorifying narrative or victimization. It involves seeing voice as part of the theorizing experience that moves to a broader politics of engagement.[28] According to Giroux, it is only in this way that pedagogy can produce citizens who are capable politically and ethically of supporting democracy and transforming the politics of assertion into one of democratic struggle. Giroux concludes, "The struggle against racism, class structures, and sexism needs to move away from being simply a language of critique, and redefine itself as part of a language of transformation and hope."[29]

There may well be elements of this description of a postmodern pedagogy that you disagree with. That is fine. Giroux, however, does raise the interesting question of how educational institutions can be agents of change rather than simply socializers for a dominant power group. Do we in church-related institutions have a prophetic role to play in this task? Should we, of anyone in higher education, assist in giving voice to the voiceless and seek ways to educate for the common good rather than merely for privilege?[30] Most of what Giroux suggests can be affirmed from the Lutheran perspective when the pedagogy is understood as historically informed and active within the world of today. (It is not intended to save us or reconcile us with God.) The need for multiple voices of discourse and exchange is a hallmark of the Lutheran dialectic, especially in its critical expression.

Giroux does not bring into the discussion the dynamics of faith that also can be a powerful basis for transformation and hope. Faith can be a powerful motivator for social change as one embodies faith commitments in daily life. (Witness the social transformation of the Reformation.) If one is pursuing the dialogue from below, then the historical claims of the Christian voice deserve to be heard among the many other voices in the conversation, without insisting that it be the final or only one. Indeed, there also is a need for serious self-criticism on the part of the Christian tradition. Exercised in a community of mutual respect and integrity, critique can be a healing and growing process. Colleges of the church should be places where one engages in such constructive dialogue and transformative pedagogy and hears the voices of the disenfranchised. Our campuses should be communities of respect and integrity where one can conduct civil discourse and debate. It is to the ethos of such a campus community that we now turn.

IV. COMMUNITY ETHOS ON CAMPUS

Noted Lutheran theologian George Forell spent virtually his entire professional life teaching in a public university setting at The University of Iowa. When asked what should be the distinguishing characteristic of the church college, he replied without hesitation, "Community."[31] One can study the Christian faith at a public university, but one cannot have the faith tradition inform the life of the academic community, bind it together, and provide a basis for care and grace among its members, all of which can occur at a college of the church. In the language of this book, church-relatedness can support a community ethos in which faith can be encountered without being imposed. That is the movement from below in which the interactions of people in the community can become windows of transcendence or windows of witness to others as they mentor them in their faith journey. This is not just the responsibility of the religion department or the campus pastor's office. They have their important and unique functions in this task, such as education in the faith traditions for the former and conduct of campus worship and outreach for the latter, but community is built by the full participation of all of its members, diverse though they may be, including those of differing faith traditions.

Community resides in trust and the willingness to transcend self-interest for the sake of the other. It is empowered by that around which the community gathers, indeed what it has in "common" to form the *communio,* the community. At our time in American society community is in short supply. Many of our students have not experienced community even at the family level, much less at the larger institutional and societal levels. As was observed earlier in Fowler's development summary, when children do not experience trustworthy care-giving, their visions of life and the world can develop into those of mistrust and fragmentation governed by survival instincts. Church colleges can provide a nurturing and supportive vision of community, one that will allow all its participants to grow and develop their potentials.

Yes, this is somewhat idealistic, but that is the point about vision. If people never have their visions elevated from the street, all they ever will see, like Plato's cave dwellers, is the surface in front of them with its cracks and two-dimensionality. We have an obligation to lift our students' vision higher and may well find our own elevated in the process. The function of the ideal, as Plato taught us, is to create a measuring rod, a canon, by which to understand our own position and from which growth can be measured. It is a form of "management by objective," if you will. If we do not have clear goals for ourselves and our community, we will not achieve anything more than self-maintenance, and even that will deteriorate over time. Our students and their families are looking for clear alternatives beyond anonymous mass production in education. The community we can nurture on our campuses is a clear alternative; while valuable in itself, this also is helpful in representing the college to others. There is thus both an intrinsic and a pragmatic rationale for the cultivation of community on our campuses. How then can we achieve it?

While all people on campus participate in and contribute to community, it is the faculty who must take the lead in its establishment and maintenance. Community cannot be assumed or taken for granted. It must be worked at continually. Faculty must be permitted enough discretionary time to allow free contact with their colleagues to build higher trust levels. To support community, faculty must trust one another enough to be willing to openly discuss community values, commitments, and faith traditions without fear of reprisal or rebuke. Community is built upon trust, whose development requires time for interpersonal contact, caring, mutual respect, and cooperation. Community requires personal self-transcendence in order to serve the common good both in and out of the classroom.

In his classic study of a community under pressure—the Japanese internment camp in China named *Shantung Compound*—Langdon Gilkey concludes that it was not the decline in physical resources that finally threatened the community's survival; instead it was the camp's inability to stop stealing from itself and to transcend self-interest enough to foster the common good. Indeed, it was what the Judeo-Christian tradition calls original sin—inordinate self-centeredness and selfishness—that nearly destroyed the community before the allied liberation. It was the spiritual and not the material values that were essential and in short supply.[32] Although we hope that our campuses are not on the edge of physical survival, the meeting of physical values can mask the absence of spiritual ones. Where will our society learn to see beyond consumption? Where will our youth be drawn out of themselves and into concern for others? Where will they experience the possibilities of true community? Yes, the church, the synagogue, the temple, and the mosque all have their important roles to play in this community formation, but they cannot fulfill educational responsibilities in the way colleges and universities can.

The liberal arts are liberating precisely because they open horizons of meaning and free the self from self-preoccupation. That has been the historic means in the Lutheran tradition to achieve the end that is the cultivation of faithful human community in the church and society. Perhaps our mission has not so much changed over the centuries as it needs a creative new instantiation on our campuses. Ethos, like the air we breathe, cannot be seen, but we cannot survive without it and we feel its invisible force. The cultivation and maintenance of this ethos of faith on our campuses is the cultivation of our spiritual environment. The spirit as well as the body needs nurture. For institutions born out of the Lutheran emphasis on incarnation to separate the spiritual from the material is to deny their birthright and forsake the integrative constructive vision of faith that they can contribute to contemporary society.

The life of faith always has involved courage and risk—and that includes the academic life of faith as well. Will we be as courageous and as willing to take risks as our predecessors whose positions we now occupy? Will we be as faithful? Our times call for new expressions and creative responses, not mere repetitions and redundancies. We do stand on the threshold of a new age for church-related higher education, and the mantle is now upon our shoulders. Undertaken in humility and faith, our tasks are achievable for we have the same spiritual resources at our disposal as did Luther and Melanchthon, Muhlenberg and Schmucker, Hauge and Walther. We simply are called to go and do likewise for our time.

QUESTIONS FOR REFLECTION

1. *How do you understand the meaning of academic freedom? Do you think that understanding is compatible with the Lutheran tradition in education?*

2. *Do you think privileging Christian presence on campus should be permitted? As a college of the church is this admissible? Required? Do you think this interferes with academic teaching or scholarly discourse?*

3. Do you agree that all thought is contextual and therefore it is better to be intentional, clear, and self-conscious about intellectual commitments?

4. What is your reaction to Giroux's pedagogical principles? Do they respond adequately to postmodern criticism? How would you implement or revise them?

5. What are the most significant factors contributing to the community ethos on your campus? Are you satisfied with that ethos?

6. What pedagogical issues and challenges to church-related higher education do you see arising in the next few years? What can your institution do to prepare itself to respond to them?

Conclusion

Perhaps it is because I have become middle-aged—but I hope it is for better reasons—that I have become aware of the importance of conserving that which is important in life. Life needs tending to, and those things that are important, if left unattended, will more than likely dissipate and die. Identity is not so much a possession as it is a process whereby one retains a continuity through time. To lose or forget one's past is not only to disconnect one from the previous identity-forming process but also to leave one without a context for addressing the future. For human beings, narrative is the formative way in which we engage time. For institutions as well as individuals this narrative is preserved as tradition. The church as well as the college exist only through the continuing instantiation of tradition as it breaks upon the crest of the wave of the present generation.

To know who we are is to know from where we have come. The understandings, experiences, histories, and conceptualities that have formed us need to be shared and transmitted, not so much as a harness by which to plow or a straightjacket to limit diversity, but as windows upon reality to allow us a vision by means of which to venture forth and return. Tradition at its best gives perspective from which to engage the novel. At its worst, tradition can refuse change and court irrelevance by retreating to some nostalgically perceived halcyon past. The challenge for both the church and the college is to maintain tradition as a compass by which to approach the future and not a lock by which to close it out!

The vision for Lutheran higher education that I have been developing would affirm meaning in the face of meaninglessness, understanding in the face of ignorance, hope in the face of despair, and life in the face of death. Our calling is to embody reflective praise through both mind and heart as they meet in the word that is voiced forth in everything from music to mathematics. For colleges/universities of the church to engage in such praise through reasoned reflection and understanding, through scholarship understood as a spiritual endeavor, through witness to the finite disclosing the infinite, and through service in meeting the needs of one's neighbor and the wider creation is to participate creatively and constructively in the mission of the church. By preparing the membership of the priesthood of all believers, they are equipping the church to constructively engage the world and, in the words of Joseph Sittler, serving "to complicate persons open."

Roland Bainton, in his widely read biography of Luther, titled *Here I Stand,* observes that the only other German to fully understand Luther was Johann Sebastian Bach.[1] Bach poured forth praise to God for justification by grace and the beauty of creation with theologically informed music in consonance with Luther's reformation insight (see Pelikan). It could be said that all of Bach's work was musical praise and that his music embodied a doxological vision of creation and redemption. It became Bach's habit to sign each work with the initials "SDG," *Soli Deo Gloria* (to God alone the glory), signifying for whom and through whom the inspiration of each work had been accomplished. It was an expression of appreciation and faith. It is my hope that we who serve in colleges of the church may do likewise, that all our lectures, papers, presentations—indeed our scholarly and community life itself—may be initialed with the "SDG." That we, too, may see our work in the context of a doxological vision like Bach's so that in all things we, too, may say, "*Soli Deo Gloria.*"

Notes

CHAPTER ONE

1. For further elaboration please see my articles "From Ethos to Logos: 'Real Presence' in the Academy," *Dialog* 36, no. 2 (spring 1997): 123–127 and "*Soli Deo Gloria:* The Doxological Tasks of the Church College," *The Cresset* (June 1995) 18–25.

2. See Mark Schwehn, chap. 2 in *Exiles from Eden* (New York: Oxford University Press, 1993).

3. Neil Postman, *The End of Education: Redefining the Value of School* (New York: Vintage Books, 1995), 7.

4. See Richard Hughes, *Models of Christian Higher Education* (Grand Rapids: Eerdman's, 1997) for more information on these approaches as well as some of the material in chap. 3.

5. See the discussion of Richard Rorty on "foundationalism" and Parker Palmer on "objectivism" in Mark Schwehn, chap. 2 in *Exiles from Eden* (New York: Oxford Univ. Press, 1993), and also works by Reuther, McFague, and Gilkey listed in the bibliography.

6. Referred to in Schwehn, *Exiles*, 25.

7. See Gregg Muilenberg, "An Aristotelian Twist to Faith and Reason," *Intersections* (summer 1997): 8.

8. Albert Gore, chap. 3 in *Earth in the Balance* (New York: Houghton Mifflin, 1992).

9. See Frederick Ferre, *Hellfire and Lightening Rods* (Maryknoll: Orbis, 1994).

10. Robert Bellah et. al., *Habits of the Heart: Individualism and Commitment in American Life* (Berkeley: University of California Press, 1985).

11. Cornel West, *Race Matters* (Boston: Beacon Press, 1993).

12. Al Gore, *Earth in the Balance* (New York: Haughton Mifflin, 1992).

13. Ibid., 12.

14. See John B. Cobb, Jr., especially chap. 10 in *The Structure of Christian Existence* (Philadelphia: Westminster Press, 1967). Nicholas Berdyaev once observed, "To eat bread is a material act, to break and share it is a spiritual one." Quoted in Langdon Gilkey, *Shantung Compound* (New York: Harper & Row, 1966), 229.

15. Ian Barbour, chap. 4 in *Religion and Science: Historical and Contemporary Issues* (San Francisco: Harper San Francisco, 1997), 77–105. See also Gregg Muilenberg, "An Aristotelian Twist to Faith and Reason," *Intersections* (summer 1997): 8–11.

16. Muilenberg, "Aristotelian Twist," 8.

17. Ibid., 9.

18. David Lotz, "Education for Citizenship in the Two Kingdoms: Reflections on the Theological Foundations of Lutheran Higher Education," in *Institutional Mission and Identity in Lutheran Higher Education* (LECNA: 1979), 7–19.

19. See Richard Hughes, *Models of Christian Higher Education* (Grand Rapids: Eerdman's, 1997) for more information on these different approaches as well as some of the material in chap. 3.

20. Ernest L. Simmons, "A Lutheran Perspective on Christian Vocation and the Liberal Arts—I," *The Cresset* (December 1988): 13–16.

21. Mark Noll, "The Lutheran Difference," *First Things* (February 1992): 31–40.

22. Ernest L. Simmons, "A Lutheran Perspective on Christian Vocation and the Liberal Arts—II," *The Cresset* (January 1989): 11–15.

23. See Luther's "The Freedom of a Christian, 1520" in *Luther's Works,* vol. 31, American ed. (Philadelphia: Muhlenberg Press, 1957), 327–77.

24. Gustaf Wingren, *Luther on Vocation* (Philadelphia: Muhlenberg Press, 1957), 180.

25. Martin Luther, To the Councilmen of All Cities in Germany that They Establish and Maintain Christian Schools, 1524," in *Luther's Works,* vol. 45 (Philadelphia: Muhlenberg Press, 1962), 347–378.

26. Stephen L. Carter, *The Culture of Disbelief* (New York: Basic Books, 1993), 3.

27. Ibid., chap. 2.

CHAPTER TWO

1. This chapter draws heavily upon the definitive study by Richard Solberg, especially chap. 14 in *Lutheran Higher Education in North America* (Minneapolis: Augsburg Publishing House, 1985), and especially chap. 1 in "*Soli Deo Gloria,* Faith and Learning in the Concordia Community: A Report to the Faculty" (Concordia College, Moorhead, Minn., 1995), co-authored by Dr. Paul Dovre, president of Concordia College, and Ernest Simmons.

2. Walther Brandt, introduction to Luther's "To the Councilmen of All Cities of Germany that They Establish and Maintain Schools," *Luther's Works,* vol. 45 (Philadelphia: Muhlenberg Press, 1962), 342.

3. *Luther's Works,* vol. 45, 347–378.

4. *Luther's Works,* vol. 46 (Philadelphia: Fortress Press, 1967), 207–258.

5. Solberg, *Lutheran Higher Education,* 14.

6. Richard Solberg, "What Can the Lutheran Tradition Contribute to Higher Education" in *Models for Christian Higher Education,* ed. Richard Hughes (Grand Rapids: Eerdmans Publishing Co., 1997), 71–81. See also Bernard Ramm, "Phillip Melanchthon: Christian Humanism" in *The Christian College in the Twentieth Century* (Grand Rapids: Eerdmans Publishing Co., 1963), 31–51.

7. Preserved Smith and Charles Jacobs, vol. 2 of *Luther's Correspondence and Other Contemporary Letters* (Philadelphia: The Lutheran Publication Society, 1913), 176, quoted in Solberg, *Lutheran Higher Education,* 17.

8. *Luther's Works,* vol. 45, 368–369.

9. Quoted in Solberg, *Lutheran Higher Education,* 18, from Einar O. Johnson, "Soli Deo Gloria: A Study of the Philosophy and Problems of Higher Education among Norwegian Lutherans in the American Environment, 1860–1960" (Ph.D. diss., University of Washington, 1966), 52.

10. David Lotz, "Education for Citizenship in the Two Kingdoms: Reflections on the Theological Foundations of Lutheran Higher Education," in *Institutional Mission and Identity in Lutheran Higher Education* (LECNA: 1979), 12.

11. Ibid., 11.

12. *Luther's Works*, vol. 1, 47–48.

13. Lotz, "Education for Citizenship," 15.

14. Theodore Tappert, trans. and ed., "The Small Catechism" in *The Book of Concord* (Philadelphia: Fortress Press, 1959), 345.

15. Noll, "Lutheran Difference," 37.

16. Sydney E. Ahlstrom, "What's Lutheran about Higher Education?—A Critique," *Papers and Proceedings of the 60th Annual Convention* (Washington, D.C.: Lutheran Educational Conference of North America, 1974), 8–16.

17. Solberg, *Lutheran Higher Education,* 20.

18. Solberg, "Lutheran Tradition," 72.

19. Ibid., 73.

20. Solberg, *Lutheran Higher Education,* 15.

21. Solberg, *Lutheran Higher Education.*

22. See Solberg, *Lutheran Higher Education,* chap. 2 "Foothold in America," for an excellent overview of the work of Muhlenberg and the founding of Lutheran colleges.

23. Eric W. Gritsch, *Fortress Introduction to Lutheranism* (Minneapolis: Fortress Press, 1994), 59. This text also provides an excellent brief overview of early Lutheran activities in North America.

24. Manning M. Patillo and Donald Mackenzie, *Church-Sponsored Higher Education in the United States: Report of the Danforth Commission* (Washington, D.C.: American Council on Education, 1966). See especially chap. 12, "Patterns of Institutional Character" for the desription of the three types of church-related undegraduate colleges in addition to the "fourth type"—the "church-related university," 191–197.

25. Quoted in William Narum, "The Tasks Ahead of Us" (presented at St. Olaf College, Northfield, Minn., 5 November 1993), ref. footnote 14.

26. Ibid., 5.

CHAPTER THREE

1. This definition, with some modification, comes from Joseph Sittler, *Essays on Nature and Grace* (Philadelphia: Fortress Press, 1972).

2. George Forell, "What's at Stake? The Place of Theology in the ELCA," *Lutheran Forum* (February 1991): 35.

3. Ernest Simmons, "A Lutheran View of Christian Vocation in the Liberal Arts—I," *The Cresset* (December, 1988): 15.

4. H. Richard Niebuhr, *Christ and Culture* (New York: Harper and Brothers, 1951), 43.

5. Forell, "What's at Stake?" 35–36.

6. K. Glenn Johnson, "The Lutheran University: Mission, Task and Focus," in *Proceedings: Lutheran Educational Conference of North America* (LECNA: 1994), 43.

7. Ibid.

8. Theodore G. Tappert, trans. and ed., *The Book of Concord* (Philadelphia: Fortress Press, 1959).

9. For much of the material in this section I am indebted to the work of Richard T. Hughes, introduction to *Models for Christian Higher Education* (Grand Rapids: Eerdmans Publishing Co., 1997), 1–9, and the presentation "The Mission of Lutheran Colleges and Universities" (the 1997 Lina R. Meyer Lecture presented at the Lutheran Educational Conference of North America [LECNA], Washington, D.C., 1 February 1997). See also "Our Place in Church-Related Higher Education in the United States," *Intersections,* no. 4 (winter 1998): 3–10.

10. "The Mission of Lutheran Colleges and Universities," 2.

11. Ibid., 3.

12. Ibid.

13. Ibid., 3–4.

14. Ibid., 4–5.

15. F. L. Cross and E. A. Livingstone, eds., "Mennonites," in *Oxford Dictionary of the Christian Church* (Oxford: Oxford University Press, 1974), 902–903.

16. Hughes, *Christian Higher Education,* 7.

17. Hughes, "The Mission of Lutheran Colleges and Universities," 6.

18. Ibid., 7.

19. Hughes, *Christian Higher Education,* 6–7.

CHAPTER FOUR

1. For more on the concept of vocation, please see Ernest Simmons, "A Lutheran View of Christian Vocation in the Liberal Arts—I and II," *The Cresset* (December 1988): 13–16 and (January 1989): 11–15.

2. Marc Kolden, "Luther on Vocation," *Word and World* III (1983):382–390.

3. *Interpreters Dictionary of the Bible,* vol. 4, ed. George Buttrick (New York: Abingdon Press, 1962), p. 791.

4. Gerhard Kittel, ed., *Theological Dictionary of the New Testament,* "klesis" vol. 3, trans. and ed. Geoffrey Bromiley (Grand Rapids: Eerdmans, 1965), 488, 491.

5. Dorothy Soelle, *To Work and to Love* (Philadelphia: Fortress Press, 1984), 16.

6. Ibid., chaps. 2–4.

7. Constance Gengenbach, "The Secularization of Vocation and the Worship of Work," *The Cresset* LI 2 (1987): 5–13.

8. Ibid., 8.

9. Kittel, *Theological Dictionary,* 492–93.

10. Martin Luther, "Lecture on Galatians," perhaps the most comprehensive single presentation of his theology. See Kolden, "Luther on Vocation," 384.

11. Gustav Wingren, *Luther on Vocation* (Philadelphia: Muhlenberg Press, 1957), 11–12.

12. See Wingren, *Luther on Vocation,* part I.

13. Kolden, "Luther on Vocation," 383.

14. Wingren, *Luther on Vocation,* 180.

15. Niebuhr, *Christ and Culture,* 179.

16. Gengenbach, "Secularization of Vocation," 10; see also the works of Weber and Tawney in the bibliography.

17. *Interpreter's Dictionary of the Bible,* "Spirit," 432–433.

18. *Interpreter's Dictionary of the Bible,* "Spiritual Body," 434.

19. *Webster's Collegiate Dictionary,* McGraw-Hill ed., s.v. "scholastic."

20. William Narum, "The Role of the Liberal Arts in Christian Higher Education," in Ditmanson et. al., *Christian Faith and the Liberal Arts* (Minneapolis: Augsburg, 1960), 3–32.

21. Lotz, "Education for Citizenship," 9.

22. Ibid., 9–10.

23. Ibid., 10.

24. Ibid., 11.

25. Gengenbach, "Secularization of Vocation," 6.

26. Narum, "Role of Liberal Arts," 4.

27. I am reminded of the horrible consequences that can occur if a dualistic separation is radically affirmed as it was by the Heaven's Gate UFO cult. They referred to their bodies as "containers" and viewed them as nonessential and dispensable as they committed mass suicide. Such neo-gnostic, Manichean dualism views the body as weak, bad, and a tomb, not as part of the goodness of creation and essential to life.

28. Frank White, *The Overview Effect: Space Exploration and Human Evolution* (Boston: Haughton Mifflin, 1987).

CHAPTER FIVE

1. James W. Fowler, *Faithful Change* (Nashville: Abingdon Press, 1996), 55–56.

2. Martin Luther, "The Large Catechism," in *The Book of Concord,* ed. Theodore Tappert (Philadelphia: Fortress Press, 1959), 365.

3. Paul Tillich, *The Dynamics of Faith* (New York: Harper Torchbook, 1958).

4. Ibid.

5. This process contributes to the philosophical position known as "foundationalism," which many postmodern thinkers, such as Richard Rorty, now seriously challenge and reject.

6. Jean Piaget, *The Psychology of Intelligence* (London: Routledge & Kegan, 1971).

7. Erik H. Erikson, *Identity, Youth and Crisis,* 1974 ed. (London: Faber & Faber, 1968).

8. Lawerence Kohlberg, "Education, Moral Development, and Faith," *Journal of Moral Education* 4, no. 1 (1974): 5–16.

9. Robert L. Selman, "The Developmental Conceptions of Interpersonal Relations," publication of the Harvard-Judge Baker Social Reasoning Project, vols. 1 and 2, 1974.

10. For critical review, see such works as *Faith Development and Fowler,* ed. Parks and Dysktra (1986), *Christian Perspectives on Faith Development,* ed. J. Astley et al. (1992), and articles such as Jardine and Viljoen "Fowler's Theory of Faith Development: An Evaluative Discussion," *Religious Education* 87, no. 1 (winter 1992): 74–85 and William O. Avery, "A Lutheran Examines James W. Fowler," *Religious Education* 85, no. 1 (winter 1990).

11. Fowler, *Faithful Change,* 56–57.

12. Ibid., 57. For an overview of the stages, see chap. 2 and his earlier work *Stages of Faith: The Psychology of Human Development and the Quest for Meaning* (San Francisco: Harper and Roe, 1981).

13. Ibid., 68.

14. Ibid., 58.

15. See the cover articles in *Time* and *Newsweek,* January 1997.

16. Fowler., *Faithful Change,* 59.

17. Ibid., 60.

18. Ibid., 61.

19. Ibid., 62.

20. Ibid.

21. Ibid., 63.

22. Ibid., 64–65.

23. Ibid., 65.

24. Ibid., 66.

25. Ibid., 67. Examples shared in a public lecture at Concordia College, Moorhead, Minn., February 1997.

26. James W. Fowler, *Stages of Faith: The Psychology of Human Development and the Quest for Meaning* (San Francisco: Harper & Row, 1981). See especially "Structural Stages and the Contents of Faith," 274–81, and the spiral diagram, 275.

27. Sharon Parks, *The Critical Years: The Young Adult Search for a Faith to Live By* (San Francisco: Harper & Row, 1986, reprint 1991).

28. Parks, *Critical Years,* 75.

29. William G. Perry, *Forms of Intellectual and Ethical Development in the College Years: A Scheme* (New York: Holt, Rinehart and Winston, 1968).

30. Parks, "The Journey Toward Mature Adult Faith: A Model," chap. 4 of *Critical Years.*

31. Ibid., 70.

32. Ibid., 53–54.

33. Quoted in Parks, *Critical Years,* 49.

34. Ibid., 49.

35. Ibid., 50.

36. Ibid.

37. Ibid., 57.

38. Ibid., 86.

39. Ibid., 101ff. See also Carol Gilligan, *In a Different Voice* (Cambridge: Harvard University Press, 1982).

40. Ibid., 105–106.

41. Ibid., 50 and 59.

42. Ibid., 84.

CHAPTER SIX

1. Lotz, "Education for Citizenship," 11.

2. Mark R. Schwehn, *Exiles from Eden: Religion and the Academic Vocation in America* (Oxford: Oxford University Press, 1993), 23–25.

3. Parker Palmer, *To Know as We Are Known: Education as a Spiritual Journey* (San Francisco: Harper San Francisco, 1993), 27.

4. Schwehn, *Exiles from Eden*, 25–26.

5. George Marsden, "The Soul of the American University: An Historical Overview," in *The Secularization of the Academy* (Oxford and New York: Oxford University Press, 1992), 38–40.

6. Robert Benne, "Recovering a Christian College: From Suspicious Tension, toward Christian Presence," *Lutheran Forum* 27 no. 2 (1993): 58–69. See also the responses of Jodock and Marshall.

7. Robert Jenson, "The Mission of the ELCA Colleges and Universities: A Theological Perspective," in *The Mission of the Evagelical Lutheran Church in America Colleges and Universities: The Joseph A. Sittler Symposium* (Chicago: ELCA, 1990), 28.

8. Manning M. Patillo and Donald Mackenzie, *Church-Sponsored Higher Education in the United States: Report of the Danforth Commission* (Washington, D.C.: American Council on Education, 1966). See especially chap. 12, "Patterns of Institutional Character" for the description of the three types of church-related undergraduate colleges in addition to the "fourth type"—the "church-related university," 191–197.

9. Ted Peters, "Culture Wars: Should Lutherans Volunteer or Be Conscripted?" *Dialog*, (winter 1993): 37–52.

10. Ibid., 39.

11. Ibid.

12. Ibid., 40.

13. Loren Meade, *The Once and Future Church* (Washington, D.C.: Alban Institute, 1991).

14. Charles C. Schroeder, "New Students, New Learning Styles," in *Change* (September/October 1993): 21–26.

15. Jenson, *Mission of ELCA Colleges*, 26.

16. Stephen Carter, *The Culture of Disbelief* (New York: Basic Books, 1993), 3.

17. Ibid., 42–43.

18. Some of the material in this section comes from "*Soli Deo Gloria* Faith and Learning in the Concordia Community: a Report to the Faculty," by the Commission on Faith and Learning, co-chaired by Paul Dovre and Ernest Simmons (Concordia College, Moorhead, Minn., 1995), "Value Reflective Education," 42–46. Gregg Muilenburg, philosophy department, Concordia College, is the primary author of this section of the report.

19. Most of the material in this section is taken from an article by Henry Giroux, "Rethinking the Boundaries of Educational Discourse: Modernism, Postmodernism, and Feminism," in Henry Giroux, *Pedagogy and the Politics of Hope: Theory, Culture and Schooling A Critical Reader* (Boulder: Westview Press, 1997).

20. Giroux, 227.

21. Ibid., 218–225.

22. Ibid., 219.

23. Ibid., 221.

24. Ibid., 222.

25. Ibid., 223.

26. Ibid., 224–225.

27. See Paulo Freire, *Pedagogy of the Oppressed* (New York: Continuum, 1982).

28. Giroux, 225

29. Ibid., 227.

30. See, for example, John Cobb and Hermon Daly, *For the Common Good: Redirecting the Economy toward Community, the Environment, and a Sustainable Future* (Boston: Beacon Press, 1989) and John B. Cobb, *Sustaining the Common Good: A Christian Perspective on the Global Economy* (Cleveland: Pilgrim Press, 1994).

31. In reply to a question at the lecture "The Vocation of a Lutheran College" (Concordia College, Moorhead, Minn., 8 April 1997).

32. Langdon Gilkey, *Shantung Compound* (New York: Harper and Row, 1966).

CONCLUSION

1. Roland Bainton, *Here I Stand* (New York: New American Library, 1978), 301.

Bibliography

Avery, William O. "A Lutheran Examines James W. Fowler." *Religious Education* 85, no. 1 (Winter 1990): 69–83.

Bainton, Roland. *Here I Stand.* New York: New American Library, 1978.

Barbour, Ian. *Religion and Science: Historical and Contemporary Issues.* San Francisco: Harper and Row, 1997.

Bellah, Robert, et. al. *Habits of the Heart: Individualism and Commitment in American Life.* Berkeley: University of California Press, 1985.

Benne, Robert. "Recovering a Christian College: From Suspicious Tension, Toward Christian Presence." *Lutheran Forum* 27, no. 2 (1993): 58–69.

Berry, Thomas. *The Dream of the Earth.* San Francisco: Sierra Club Books, 1988.

———. "Religion in the Ecological Era." American Academy of Religion Plenary Lecture, Washington D.C., 22 November 1993.

Boyer, Ernest. "Teaching Religion in the Public Schools and Elsewhere." *Journal of the American Academy of Religion* LX, no. 3 (1992): 515–524.

Burtchaell, James. "The Decline and Fall of the Christian College." *First Things* (April 1991a): 16–29.

———. "The Decline and Fall of the Christian College (II)." *First Things* (May 1991b): 30–38.

Carter, Stephen. *The Culture of Disbelief.* New York: Basic Books, 1993.

Cobb, John B. *The Structure of Christian Existence.* Philadelphia: Westminster Press, 1967.

———. *Becoming a Thinking Christian.* Nashville: Abingdon Press, 1993.

———. *Sustaining the Common Good: A Christian Perspective on the Global Economy.* Cleveland: Pilgrim Press, 1994.

Cuninggim, Merrimon. *Uneasy Partners: The College and the Church.* Nashville: Abingdon Press, 1994.

Daly, Hermon E. and John B. Cobb, Jr. *For the Common Good: Redirecting the Economy toward Community, the Environment, and a Sustainable Future.* Boston: Beacon Press, 1989.

De Jong, Arthur. *Reclaiming a Mission: New Direction for the Church–Related College.* Grand Rapids: Eerdmans Publishing Co, 1990.

Ditmanson, Harold, Howard Hong, and Warren Quanbeck, eds. *Christian Faith and the Liberal Arts.* Minneapolis: Augsburg Publishing House, 1960.

Erikson, Erik H., ed. *Identity, Youth and Crisis.* London: Faber & Faber, 1974.

Forell, George. "Reflections on the Task of Colleges and Seminaries." Paper presented at Region III planning conference at Luther Northwestern Theological Seminary, 16 June 1993.

Fowler, James W. *Stages of Faith: The Psychology of Human Development and the Quest for Meaning.* San Francisco: Harper & Row Publishers, 1981.

———. *Faith Development and Pastoral Care.* Philadelphia: Fortress Press, 1987.

———. *Faithful Change.* Nashville: Abingdon Press, 1996.

Freire, Paulo. *Pedagogy of the Oppressed.* New York: Continuum, 1982.

Gengenbach, Constance. "The Secularization of Vocation and the Worship of Work." *The Cresset* LI, no. 2 (1987): 5–13.

———. "Academic Life: Vocation or Career?" *The Cresset* LI, no. 3 (1988): 5–12.

———, ed. "Faith, Learning and the Church College: Addresses by Joseph Sittler." St. Olaf College, Northfield, Minn., 1989.

Gilkey, Langdon. *Shantung Compound.* New York: Harper & Row Publishers, 1966.

———. "Human Sustainability in a Nature that Is Mortal." AAR Theology and Science Group Paper, Washington D.C., 22 November 1993.

Gilligan, Carol. *In a Different Voice: Psychological Theory and Women's Development.* Cambridge: Harvard University Press, 1982.

Giroux, Henry A. *Pedagogy and the Politics of Hope: Theory, Culture and Schooling a Critical Reader.* Boulder: Westview Press, a Division of Harper Collins, 1997.

Gore, Al. *Earth in the Balance.* New York: Haughton Mifflin, 1992.

Gritsch, Eric. W. *Fortress Introduction to Lutheranism.* Minneapolis: Fortress Press, 1994.

Hall, Douglas John. *God and Human Suffering.* Minneapolis: Augsburg Press, 1986.

Hauerwas, Stanley and John Westerhoff, eds. *Schooling Christians: Holy Experiments in American Education.* Grand Rapids: Eerdmans Publishing Co., 1992.

Hirsch, E. D. *Cultural Literacy: What Every American Needs to Know.* Boston: Houghton Mifflin, 1987.

Holmes, Arthur F. *The Idea of a Christian College,* rev. ed. Grand Rapids: Eerdmans Publishing Co., 1987.

Hughes, Richard T. "Our Place in Church-Related Higher Education in the United States." *Intersections* 4 (winter 1998): 3–10.

Hughes, Richard T. and William B. Adrian, eds. *Models for Christian Higher Education: Strategies for Survival and Success in the Twenty–First Century.* Grand Rapids: Eerdmans Publishing Co., 1997.

Hunter, James Davison. *Culture Wars: The Struggle to Define America.* New York: Basic Books, 1991.

Huntington, Samuel P. "The Clash of Civilizations?" *Foreign Affairs* (Summer 1993): 22–49.

IDB. George Buttrick, ed. *The Interpreter's Dictionary of the Bible.* Vol. 4. New York: Abingdon Press, 1962.

Jardine, Marlene M. and Henning G. Viljoen. "Fowler's Theory of Faith Development: An Evaluative Discussion." *Religious Education* 87, no. 1 (winter 1992): 74–85.

Jenson, Robert. "On the Renewing of the Mind." *The Cresset* LI, no. 4 (1988): 10–16.

———. "The Mission of the ELCA Colleges and Universities: A Theological Perspective." The Mission of the Evangelical Lutheran Church in America Colleges and Universities: The Joseph A. Sittler Symposium. Chicago: ELCA, 1990.

Johnson, Benton, Dean R. Hoge, and Donald A. Luidens. "Mainline Churches: The Real Reason for Decline." *First Things* (March 1993): 13–18.

Kegan, Robert. *The Evolving Self: Problem and Process in Human Development.* Cambridge: Harvard University Press, 1982.

Kittel, Gerhard, ed. *Theological Dictionary of the New Testament.* Edited and translated by Geoffrey Bromiley. Grand Rapids: Eerdmans. *Klesis* 3, 1965.

Kohlberg, Lawerence. "Education, Moral Development and Faith." *Journal of Moral Education* 4, no. 1 (1974): 5–16.

Kolden, Marc. "Luther on Vocation." *Word and World* III (1983): 382–390.

Lotz, David. "Education for Citizenship in the Two Kingdoms: Reflections on the Theological Foundations of Lutheran Higher Education." *Institutional Mission and Identity in Lutheran Higher Education.* LECNA (1979): 7–19.

Luther, Martin. "To the Councilmen of All Cities in Germany that They Establish and Maintain Christian Schools," 1524. *Luther's Works* 45:339–378, Philadelphia: Muhlenberg Press, 1962.

———. "A Sermon on Keeping Children in School," 1530. *Luther's Works* 46:207–258, Philadelphia: Fortress Press, 1967.

Marsden, George. "The Soul of the American University: An Historical Overview." In *The Secularization of the Academy.* Oxford and New York: Oxford University Press, 1992.

———. "Theology and the University: Newman's Idea and Current Realities." In *The Idea of the University,* John Henry Newman. New Haven: Yale University Press, 1996 reprint.

———. *The Outrageous Idea of Christian Scholarship.* New York: Oxford University Press, 1997.

Marty, Martin. "The Changing Role of Religion in Higher Education." In *Religion and Higher Education, 1989 Paine Lectures in Religion,* edited by Joel P. Brereton and Patricia A. Love. Columbia: University of Missouri Press, 1989.

McFague, Sallie. *The Body of God: An Ecological Theology.* Minneapolis: Fortress Press, 1993.

Meade, Loren. *The Once and Future Church.* Washington, D.C.: Alban Institute, 1991.

Moltmann, Jurgen. "The Crucified God." *Theology Today* 31 (1974): 6–18.

Narum, William. "The Role of the Liberal Arts in Christian Higher Education." In *Christian Faith and the Liberal Arts,* Ditmanson et al. Minneapolis: Augsburg, 1960, pp. 3–32.

———. "The Tasks Ahead of Us." Presented at St. Olaf College, Northfield, Minn., 5 November 1993.

Nelson, John Oliver, ed. *Work and Vocation.* New York: Harper Bros., 1954.

Niebuhr, H. Richard. *Christ and Culture.* New York: Harper and Row, 1951.

Noll, Mark. "The Lutheran Difference." *First Things* (February 1992):31–40.

Nussbaum, Martha C. *Cultivating Humanity: A Classical Defense of Reform in Liberal Education.* Cambridge: Harvard University Press, 1997.

Olsen, Arthur, ed. *The Quest for a Viable Saga: The Church-Related College in an Age of Pluralism.* Valparaiso: Association of Lutheran College Faculty, 1977.

Palmer, Parker. *To Know as We Are Known: Education as a Spiritual Journey.* San Francisco: Harper San Francisco, 1993.

Pannenberg, Wolfhart. *Toward a Theology of Nature: Essays on Science and Faith.* Louisville: Westminster/John Knox Press, 1993.

Parks, Sharon. "Cognitive and Ethical Growth: The Making of Meaning." In *The Modern American College,* edited by Arthur Chickering. San Francisco: Jossy-Bass, 1981.

———. *The Critical Years: The Young Adult Search for a Faith to Live By.* New York: Harper and Row Publishers, 1986.

Parks, Sharon and Craig Dysktra. *Faith Development and Fowler.* San Francisco: Harper & Roe Publishers, 1986.

Pattillo, Manning M. and Donald M. Mackenzie. *Church-Sponsored Higher Eduation in the United States: Report of the Danforth Commission.* Washington, D.C.: American Council on Education, 1966.

Pelikan, Jaroslav. *Bach Among the Theologians.* Philadelphia: Fortress Press, 1986.

———. *The Idea of the University: A Reexamination.* New Haven: Yale University Press, 1992.

Perry, William G. *Forms of Intellectual and Ethical Development in the College Years: A Scheme.* New York: Holt, Rinehart and Winston, 1968.

Peters, Ted. "Culture Wars: Should Lutherans Volunteer or Be Conscripted?" *Dialog* (Winter 1993): 37–52.

Piaget, Jean. *The Psychology of Intelligence.* London: Routledge & Kegan, 1971.

Postman, Neil. *The End of Education: Redefining the Value of School.* New York: Vintage Books, 1995.

Quanbeck, Warren. "The Theological Basis of Christian Higher Education." In *Christian Faith and the Liberal Arts.* Edited by Harold H. Ditmanson and Howard V. Hong. Minneapolis: Augsburg Publishing, 1960.

Ramm, Bernard. *The Christian College in the Twentieth Century.* Grand Rapids: Eerdmans Publishing Company, 1963.

Ruether, Rosemary Radford. *Gaia and God: An Ecofeminist Theology of Earth Healing.* San Francisco: Harper San Francisco, 1992.

Schroeder, Charles C. "New Students—New Learning Styles." *Change* (September/October 1993): 21–26.

Schwehn, Mark R. *Exiles from Eden: Religion and the Academic Vocation in America.* Oxford: Oxford University Press, 1993.

Simmons, Ernest L. "A Lutheran Perspective on Christian Vocation and the Liberal Arts—I." *The Cresset* (December 1988): 13–16.

———. "A Lutheran Perspective on Christian Vocation and the Liberal Arts—II." *The Cresset* (January 1989): 11–15.

———. "From Ethos to Logos: 'Real Presence' in the Academy." *Dialog* 36, no. 2 (spring 1997): 123–127.

Sittler, Joseph. *Essays on Nature and Grace.* Philadelphia: Fortress Press, 1972.

———. "Church Colleges and the Truth." In "Faith, Learning and the Church College: Addresses by Joseph Sittler." St. Olaf College, Northfield, Minn., 1989.

Soelle, Dorothy. *To Work and to Love: A Theology of Creation.* Minneapolis: Fortress Press, 1984.

Solberg, Richard. *Lutheran Higher Education in North America.* Minneapolis: Augsburg Publishing House, 1985.

"*Soli Deo Gloria* Faith and Learning in the Concordia Community: A Report to the Faculty." By The Commission on Faith and Learning, cochaired by Paul Dovre and Ernest Simmons. Concordia College, Moorhead, Minn., 1995.

Tappert, Theodore G., trans. and ed. *The Book of Concord.* Philadelphia: Fortress Press, 1959.

Tawney, R. H. *Religion and the Rise of Capitalism.* New York, 1962.

Wainwright, Geoffrey. *Doxology: The Praise of God in Worship, Doctrine and Life, a Systematic Theology.* New York: Oxford University Press, 1980.

Weber, Max. *Protestant Ethic and the Spirit of Capitalism.* New York: Scribners, 1958.

West, Cornel. *Race Matters.* Boston: Beacon Press, 1993.

White, Frank. *The Overview Effect: Space Exploration and Human Evolution.* Boston: Haughton Mifflin, 1987.

Whitehead, Alfred North. *The Aims of Education.* New York: Free Press, 1957.

Wingren, Gustaf. *Luther on Vocation.* Philadelphia: Muhlenberg Press, 1957.

Woodward, Kenneth L. "Dead End for the Mainline?" *Newsweek,* 9 August 1993, 46–48.